HOUSE
PROUD

HOUSE

MERCER UNIVERSITY PRESS | MACON, GEORGIA

PROUD

A SOCIAL HISTORY OF ATLANTA INTERIORS, 1880-1919

LORI ERIKSEN RUSH

MUP/H883

© 2014 Mercer University Press
1400 Coleman Avenue
Macon, Georgia 31207
All rights reserved

First Edition

Book design by Burt&Burt

Books published by Mercer University Press are printed on acid-free paper that meets the
requirements of the American National Standard for Information Sciences—
Permanence of Paper for Printed Library Materials.

Mercer University Press is a member of Green Press Initiative (greenpressinitiative.org),
a nonprofit organization working to help publishers and printers increase their use
of recycled paper and decrease their use of fiber derived from endangered forests.
This book is printed on recycled paper.

ISBN 978-0-88146-476-4

Cataloging-in-Publication Data is available from the Library of Congress

In memory of my parents,
Marge and Norman Eriksen

PREFACE

This study began with a bequest to me from a former student: a small box of slides containing images of nineteenth-century Atlanta interiors. As I searched for additional information about the city's design history, it became evident that while Atlanta's architecture had been the subject of numerous books, the interiors of its nineteenth- and early twentieth-century homes and the lives they supported remained relatively unexplored.

My research into Atlanta interiors began with interviews with long-time Atlanta interior designers. It was during an interview with the dean of Atlanta interior design, the late T. Gordon Little, that I discovered a recurring theme in the story of Atlanta homes. When I asked his opinion of the Atlanta interiors market, he replied, "Atlanta is house proud." His observation intrigued me, and I began to question how the city's pride in its homes originally developed. It was in the written and visual records of post-Civil War Atlanta homes that I found the story of this "house-proud" city.

The greatest single source of written information about Atlanta's nineteenth-century interiors is the city's newspapers. Descriptions of interiors, furniture, treatments, and color schemes filled the Sunday society pages and magazine sections. Articles listing new homes being built in Atlanta provided information regarding interior finishes and materials, stylistic designations, and custom detailing. But the most insightful information came from the architects and writers of home-advice articles, who spoke with unflinching candor about the quality, or lack thereof, of interior decoration in the homes of their day.

As the greatest number of photographs comes from the period 1880–1919, I confined my study to those years. Of the photographs of interiors that remain, most are of the homes of prominent Atlanta business, social, and political leaders. It is regrettable that so few photographs of more modest homes have survived, as they would have provided a more complete visual record of how the majority of nineteenth-century Atlantans actually lived.

FACING PAGE: *Fig. A* PARLOR, WILLIS E. AND ANNA RAGAN RESIDENCE, CA. 1895

Regarding the evolution of the profession of interior decoration, I feel an explanation may be in order. The title "interior decorator" has been used throughout the text. It is an appellation that is an anathema to anyone familiar with the interior design profession's decades-long struggle for recognition and fails to accurately represent the complex work performed by trained professionals today. But during the years covered by this study, it was the title in common use and was more or less an accurate description of the services provided. By the mid-twentieth century, the term "interior designer" emerged as the title of choice among trained professionals. It is now the title used by professional organizations and, in many states, one that is recognized by law.

The home adds another dimension to our understanding of society as seen in its most intimate setting. My aim is to provide insights into Atlanta, its people, its culture, and the times through a study of the trappings with which nineteenth-century Atlantans surrounded themselves in their homes. If *House Proud* spurs further inquiry and a renewed interest in documenting Atlanta's early interiors, my time will have been well spent.

ACKNOWLEDGEMENTS

My observations regarding the nineteenth-century American home are based on the work of several authors whose notable research into the material culture of the home helped shape my understanding of the powerful connection people have with home and possessions: Dr. Kenneth Ames, Dr. Clifford Edward Clark, Jr., Dr. Thomas Schlereth, and Thorstein Veblen. Franklin Garrett's indispensible *Atlanta and Environs: A Chronicle of Its People and Events, 1880s–1930s* provided the framework for Atlanta's historical context. Civil War journals, such as Sallie Clayton's *Requiem for a Lost City: Sallie Clayton's Memoirs of Civil War Atlanta and the Old South* and Eliza Frances Andrews's *The War-Time Journal of a Georgia Girl, 1864–1865*, provided insight into the psychological toll the war had on civilians in Atlanta. Mary Raoul Millis's *The Family of Raoul: A Memoir* and her unpublished autobiography presented a glimpse into upper-class Atlanta society at the end of the nineteenth century.

As the majority of the primary resources used in my research came from the Atlanta History Center, I am indebted to the staff of the Kenan Research Center for always coming to my aid. I am especially grateful to Paige Adair for her excellent work on the images, among which were several from Walter T. Downing's 1897 publication, *Domestic Architecture*. I also want to acknowledge the staff of the Manuscript, Archive, and Rare Book Library of the Robert W. Woodruff Library at Emory University; Gail De Loach of the Visual Materials Reference department of the Georgia Archives; Marianne Bradley of the McCain Library at Agnes Scott College; Debbie Thompson of Brenau University; and Crystal Butts of the Georgia Trust for Historic Preservation for their help in acquiring additional photographs; and the staff of Mercer University Press for patiently walking me through the process. I also want to thank Sonny Clark for his images and help in getting information about his aunt, May Belle Clark, and those who supplied photographs of their family homes: Katherine Cox Dickey Marbut for the photographs of the James Dickey Jr. home, and Ralph Ragan Morrison for the parlor of the Willis E. Ragan home.

I am deeply grateful to the people who read the manuscript and whose comments and input I value beyond words: Dr. Gordon May, Jeff Ashworth, Bonnie Bailey, Boyd Coons, and Dr. Hester Lee Fury. I especially want to acknowledge Kitty Farnham, who has gone above and beyond in support of "House Proud." Her infectious enthusiasm, generosity of spirit, and energy expended on behalf of this project have earned my eternal gratitude.

There are those for whom my thanks come too late: my former student, the late Frank Glenn, for the box of slides of Atlanta interiors that sparked this inquiry; the late interior designer T. Gordon Little, who gave me the idea for the title of the book; and my friend and mentor, the late Dr. Tim Bookout, for enriching my life with his vast knowledge of antiques, unerring design judgment, and his sorely missed sense of humor.

There is one person to whom I owe a debt I cannot repay: my friend and colleague, Dr. Claire May. From the first rough draft, she has been an insightful critic and tireless editor of the manuscript. Without her wise council, encouragement, and belief in the project, I question whether this book would have ever seen the light of day. Thank you, Claire.

Finally, I thank my family for their support and patience: my husband, Greg, and our daughters, Regan and Ashley. And to my grandchildren, Rowan, Lofton, and Oliver, my thanks for keeping me focused on the future rather than the past.

Thank You

My heartfelt gratitude goes to those individuals whose generosity made *House Proud* possible. This book could not have been published without your support.

Mr. and Mrs. Bonneau Ansley Jr.
Mr. and Mrs. Shepard Bryan Ansley
Jeff Ashworth
Mr. and Mrs. Charles Coleman Benedict
Mr. and Mrs. Thomas Cobb Benedict
Mr. and Mrs. Shepard Bryan Benedict
Mr. and Mrs. William Noble Benedict Jr.
Jane Cocke Black
Nancy Carter Bland
Rodney Mims Cook Jr.
Mr. and Mrs. Stephen K. Critchfield
Margaret Perdue Denny
Harriet Witham Ellis
Kitty and Clayton Farnham
Lillian R. Gantsoudes
Alston Glenn
Mr. and Mrs. Henry W. Grady
Mr. and Mrs. W. Barrett Howell
Baxter, Jiong, and Sophie Jones
Douglas, Judy, and Bates Jones
Julia Lowry Jones
David L. Perdue
A. Rhodes Perdue
Lillian Deakins Timberlake

HOUSE
PROUD

PROLOGUE

Photographs of late nineteenth-century Atlanta interiors confirm a similarity between homes of the North and South unknown before the Civil War. But beneath the fashionable veneer of postwar Atlanta homes, invisible to the camera, lay vestiges of regional attitudes that sprang from a centuries-old reservoir of traditions, values, and beliefs, and the more recent experience of humiliation and loss. These attitudes lent a Southern nuance to the national understandings of "home." Thus, any discussion of the Atlanta home must begin by pointing out a few peculiarly Southern associations with the term.

The antebellum home was the setting for all aspects of Southern existence, from the intimacy of its domestic life to its public and social interactions and the economy that sustained it. The home was the locus of a Southern subculture, which, from colonial times, had developed largely in response to shared experiences of an agrarian context and economic dependence on slavery. From subsistence farmers to wealthy planters whose lives of leisure were built on the forced labor of others, Southerners shared common values beginning with a bone-deep affinity with the land and sense of pride in having beaten nature and the odds.

The remote locations of farms and plantations fostered self-sufficiency and reliance on a large family network. Difficulty of travel made hospitality both a social and a humanitarian necessity. Isolation resulted in a culture of permanence that valued tradition and continuity, one in which land, homes, and possessions were inherited along with a heightened sense of familial pride and an almost sacred sense of heritage and place. For Southerners who were born, lived, and died in the same house as their ancestors, the home was a symbol of a revered way of life, one they were determined to defend.

By the end of the Civil War in 1865, Southern culture was in crisis. The Southern way of life that had taken over two centuries to evolve had taken only four years to dismantle. The bitterness, resentment, and shame engendered by the defeat and years of punishing reconstruction left a stain on the Southern psyche that remained for generations. The epoch of the Old South passed into memory along with many of the homes that had become its emblem. Decades later, as Southerners wrote about their homes before the war, pages brimmed with a profound sense of loss.

These were some of the memories and experiences carried by the Southerners among the postwar generation of Atlanta leaders. But remarkably, somewhere along the way to their future, Atlantans managed to leave their heaviest baggage behind. They seemed to understand that the past could inspire and enlighten, burden or confine; it could be a place of refuge and a place to visit, but there was a danger in lingering there too long. Along with a New South, Atlantans created a new model of the Southern home, contemporary in style and fully in accord with emerging national notions about the meaning of home and possessions. Brash and new, Atlanta and its finest homes fully embraced the spirit of the age, with its delight in technology, novelty, consumption, and display. And while that home might be the visual antithesis of classic, Old South notions of elegance and refined taste, in their lives and lifestyles Atlantans continued to honor memories and traditions salvaged from their past. It is within the confluence of national influences and regional memory that the story of the late nineteenth-century Atlanta interior unfolds.

THE JOHN H. AND SUSAN LEONARD JAMES MANSION

(GEORGIA GOVERNOR'S MANSION)

"The Finest Residence in Georgia"

Atlanta Constitution, 25 December 1869

orn in 1830 in Henry County, Georgia, John James came to Atlanta in 1850. A self-described gambler, he began his career selling everything from whiskey and books to jewelry. Unlike most of his contemporaries, James sat out the Civil War in Nassau, returning to the city at the conflict's end. Capitalizing on the energy and possibilities of postwar Atlanta, James settled into a lucrative career in private banking. By 1869, when he built his impressive mansion on Peachtree, James was a wealthy man.[14]

James's grand residence was as conspicuous as his new money could buy. Designed by Atlanta architect William H. Parkins, the house featured the latest in plumbing technology with hot and cold water, bathrooms, and separate water closets. Inside blinds (shutters) folded into wall panels that flanked the double, thick "French" quality windows. The interior detailing included oiled and varnished black walnut and oak trim and enameled slate mantels.[15] James filled the home with ornate furniture, which he later boasted "was the handsomest made in those days."[16] A year after James completed the building of his new home, he sold the completely furnished house to the state of Georgia for use as the Governor's Mansion.

In 1883, the home went through a renovation that took three months to complete. The interior finishing, painting, and frescos were the work of an Atlanta interior decorating company, Pause & Schroeter (later; Pause, Schroeter & Co.). Unlike the technique of painting on wet plaster, the term

---

[14] E. C. Bruffey, "John H. James: For Half a Century a Central Figure in Atlanta's History," *Atlanta Constitution*, 19 February 1911, 10.

[15] "A Fine Specimen of Architecture," *Daily Constitution*, 10 April 1869, 3.

[16] "The First Mansion," *Atlanta Constitution*, 4 November 1888, 5.

Fig. I.1   THE "RED PARLOR," GOVERNOR'S MANSION, CA. 1894

"fresco" loosely referred to any painted wall decoration, usually done on canvas and then applied to the wall. The carpet and the design of the frescos, ceiling, and wall treatments in the house's two parlors were identical with the exception of the color schemes. In the parlor to the left of the entry, all drapery and upholstery fabrics were a deep red. Beneath an elaborately painted ceiling was a frieze painted in a dark-hued arabesque pattern. To the right of the entry was the "Blue Parlor." With its more muted color scheme, it was described by the *Atlanta Constitution* as the "handsomer" of the two. Among the furnishings were a number of carved rosewood pieces brought from the old Governor's Mansion at Milledgeville.[17]

[17] "Repairs at the Mansion," *Atlanta Constitution*, 30 December 1883, 6.

Under the direction of Governor William J. Northen's wife, Martha Neel Northen, the mansion underwent another renovation in 1894. Figure I.1 shows the "Red Parlor" with its newly decorated frieze and electric lighting, cleverly disguised within the rosettes just below the cornice molding. Early electric light was weak and necessitated a greater number of bulbs to achieve the necessary lighting levels. The "Blue Parlor," figure I.2, with its sumptuously upholstered chairs and display of art, including sculpture on a pedestal and paintings, created a more feminine ambiance. The state's house now stood ready to welcome the world at the Cotton States and International Exposition the following year.

This celebrated house, built and furnished with such pride, survived for only fifty years. Heavy use and deferred maintenance finally took their toll both structurally and on the once elegant interior. The house was closed in 1921 and its furniture sold at auction in February of the following year. According to the *Atlanta Constitution*, items sold included "several large mirrors, [a] parlor suite,... settees and chairs, rugs,... and a sideboard which was brought down from the attic." Many pieces found a home in the new Atlanta chapter house of the United Daughters of the Confederacy (UDC), where, along with other relics of the Confederacy, they remained revered tokens of the region's past. [18]

John James built several more houses in Atlanta, and while his business life in later years was marked by both success and failure, he nevertheless survived to earn the respect of the city and the moniker the "Jay Gould" of Atlanta.[19] James died in 1917.

[18] "Half Century of State History Recalled in Sale," *Atlanta Constitution*, 15 February 1922, 13.
[19] Bruffey, "John H. James," 10.

perceptions to national beliefs regarding wealth, class, gender, and, to a lesser degree, race, Atlanta interiors spoke to national tastes and attitudes with a Southern accent.

CLASS MATTERS

In Atlanta, as with most of the country, class was defined by one's financial statement, not one's antecedents. In its homes, Atlanta's socioeconomic distinctions were immediately recognizable. From the home's address to the quality, cost, and source of its furnishings and the level of professional assistance employed in its design, Atlanta homes were unmistakable indicators of the owner's position in the city's social and economic pecking order.

Homes of the Middle Class. Period descriptions and images of more modest middle-class Atlanta homes in the late nineteenth century are relatively rare in comparison with written accounts and photographs of grander residences. Before the widespread use of the Kodak camera, photographs were normally taken outdoors or in studios. Most middle-class Atlantans would have had neither the money nor the motivation to hire a professional to photograph their surroundings. The few photographs of middle-class interiors that have survived show homes designed to meet the everyday needs of the family's domestic life. The chief design criteria for these homes were convenience and comfort. While some are sparsely furnished with only the most utilitarian items, others suggest homes whose owners were not without pretensions or awareness of trends. Their attempts at refinement and fashion met with mixed success, but their interiors were nonetheless models of the nineteenth-century ideal of middle-class domesticity: respectability, gentility, and comfort. Their interior selections reflect individual tastes unchecked by professional influences. With their lack of stylish veneer, they provide an honest, less affected insight into the home life lived by the majority of Atlantans at the end of the nineteenth century.

The interior photographs of the Crescent Avenue home of music teacher Henry Howell and his wife, Nellie, figure 2.1, offer a rare, intimate glimpse of middle-class Atlantans at home. In figure 2.2, the Howells are

Fig. 2.1 EXTERIOR. HENRY AND NELLIE HOWELL RESIDENCE

seen in their modest parlor spending a quiet evening together. Nellie strikes a contemplative pose on the Turkish divan while the family source of income, the piano, stands in the background. Above the piano, images of great composers are displayed on the wall. In figure 2.3, the same room seen from another angle captures the couple reading by their newly installed electricity. Before electric lighting, tubes attached to gas ceiling fixtures provided fuel for table lamps. As shown here, during the transition to electricity, original gas fixtures were retrofitted to accommodate the new technology. With its plain walls and windows simply treated with shades for privacy and a gauzy, thin curtain, the Howell's parlor made few concessions to fashion. In the dining room, figure 2.4, the furnishings are modest examples of current trends: the geometrically patterned portières in the doorway and the Eastern-style rug lying at an angle on the floor are features of the Turkish "taste"; the shelf, with its simply arranged display of family china and the pillar-and-scroll table, suggest the Colonial Revival influence.

HOUSE
PROUD

Fig. 2.2 PARLOR, HENRY AND NELLIE HOWELL RESIDENCE, CA. 1897

Popular and inexpensive solutions to seating, Bentwood chairs, with their painted finish and caned seats, were an early example of well-designed, mass-produced furniture, with no pseudo-historical reference.

✦ *Homes of the Upwardly Mobile.* The luxury arts, such as elegant interiors, had traditionally been the concern of those in society who could afford them. While most nineteenth-century reformers took their campaign to the vast American middle class, society editors and writers such as Edith Wharton and Ogden Codman Jr., authors of *The Decoration of Houses* (1897), reinforced the commonly held idea that interior decoration was the exclusive province of the rich.

Writing for the *Atlanta Constitution* in the 1890s and early years of the twentieth century, Isma Dooly (figure 2.5) represented the local society woman's view of the interior. In her articles, interiors served as settings for the elegant lifestyle of Atlanta's glitterati, the social elect whose homes were

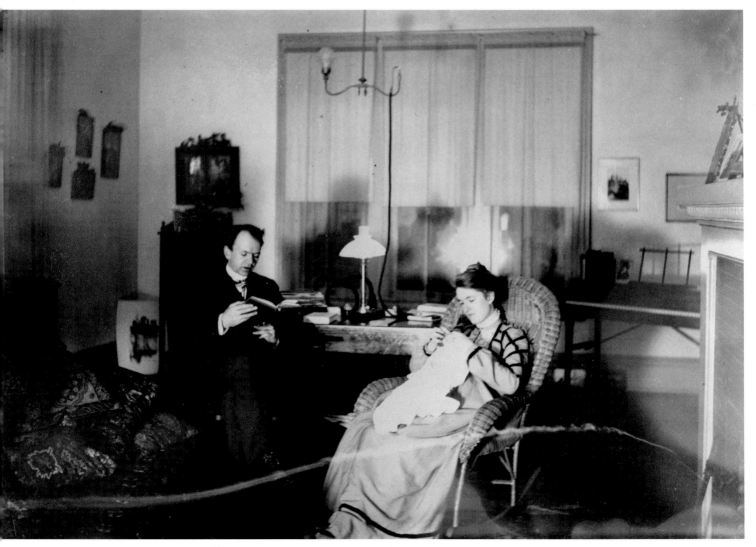

Fig. 2.3   PARLOR, HENRY AND NELLIE HOWELL RESIDENCE, 1897

Fig. 2.5 ISMA DOOLY, 1895

the pride of the city and whose entertainments, fashions, and interiors were of keen interest to readers. For the middle class, they were the standard to emulate and for their peers, to surpass.

To Dooly, featured interiors were always "artistic," "cultured," and "refined." However, amid the superlatives of her journalistic prose, valuable descriptions emerged regarding color, fabric, and furniture styles of Atlanta's finest homes, accompanied by photographs of the interiors and the women who presided over them.

Many of the surviving photos of Atlanta's most fashionable homes come through the lens of one of the city's leading nineteenth-century photographers, F. L. Howe. For decades he, along with others, documented the assets and lifestyles of some of the city's most prominent citizens. Of special significance to the history of Atlanta interiors are his photographs published in W. T. Downing's *Domestic Architecture* (1897). The photographic evidence combined with written nineteenth-century descriptions indicates that the city's finest homes featured interiors that were accurate, if conventional, reflections of their late nineteenth-century milieu. Atlanta interiors, though hardly comparable to those found on New York's Fifth Avenue or the opulent summer "cottages" of Newport, Rhode Island, were nonetheless fine examples of what was fashionable in their day.

THE SOCIAL HOUSE

In *The House Beautiful*, Clarence Cook differentiated between homes designed for the domestic life of the family and homes designed for the social life, where the needs of the family were subordinated to the expectations of society.[24] In the organization of the plan and selection and layout of furnishings, Atlanta's most fashionable homes supported the formalized social rituals that governed the lives of the upper class and those in the middle class with higher aspirations. The deft performance of these rites within a stylish yet tasteful setting identified one as a person of breeding

---

[24] Clarence Cook, *The House Beautiful: Essays on Beds and Tables, Stools and Candlesticks* (New York: Scribner, Armstrong and Company, 1878), 47. http://www.archive.org/details/housebeautiful00cookgoog.

FACING PAGE: *Fig. 2.4* DINING ROOM, HENRY AND NELLIE HOWELL RESIDENCE, CA. 1897

and refinement. These qualities would have taken on heightened importance for a city anxious to project an image of social and cultural sophistication while carrying on the South's reputation as the epitome of manners and gracious living. Furthermore, entertainment of visitors in the South was considered an almost sacred responsibility, and one's ability to do it well, a social imperative.

The social house supported a wide variety of entertainments. A list of these social functions, culled from the society pages of the city's newspapers, included routine afternoon calls, luncheons, teas, receptions, dinners, musical events, and balls. The social house also served as the setting for life's rites of passage—christenings, debuts, weddings, and funerals. Every member of Atlanta's "400" gave at least one social event each year. As with everything of fashion, wealthy Atlanta women looked to the North for inspiration, traveling to New York and Boston to purchase the finest in dress and furnishings and to enjoy the latest in entertainments of the social season.

Photos of elegantly dressed diners at lavish dinner parties, such as those pictured in figure 2.6, were common in Atlanta. What is less usual, however, is the inclusion in the photo of four tuxedoed servants standing behind the diners on the right. The result is a rare tableau of Atlanta's social hierarchy as expressed in an upper-class household.

✈ *The Hierarchal Home.* The plan of the Samuel M. Inman house, figure 2.7, illustrates how the highly compartmentalized, upper-class Atlanta home reinforced the social order and its protocols. At the top of the home's hierarchy was the first floor, which contained the ceremonial spaces designed to facilitate the evening's entertainments. From a small vestibule guests entered the large central hall around which the public rooms were located. The circulation moved easily from the reception room to the parlor and on to the dining room. Centered at the end of the hall, the dining room was the ceremonial epicenter of the Inman home; its visibility on entering the house heightened guests' anticipation of the delights to come. The less formal sitting room and library were to the right. Mr. Inman's library was accompanied by a den and bath. Other rooms found in upscale Atlanta homes included music rooms, tea rooms, breakfast rooms, conservatories,

Fig. 2.8   Entry hall, Samuel and Mildred Inman residence, 1897

Fig. 2.10   PARLOR, SAMUEL AND MILDRED INMAN RESIDENCE, 1897

complete in itself."[34] The Inman parlor, shown in figure 2.10, exemplifies
the effect Wheeler described and is an unmistakable example of the parlor's
feminine and artistic associations. Paneling and trim of old ivory frame
patterned walls. Prominently displayed between the windows, sculpture on
a pedestal confirms the artistic nature of the parlor. Centrally located, the
tufted tête-à-tête provides a pivot around which assorted seating allows
guests to arrange themselves in small groups during social functions. A
gilded Louis XV table sits at an angle in the corner. By the 1890s, the French
styles, gilded or painted Louis XV and Louis XVI, were the overwhelming
favorites among Atlanta women. Small-scale, lightweight occasional pieces
such as chairs, tables, and stools were mixed with wicker, as well as plush,
upholstered love seats, armchairs, and benches decorated with fringe and
ruffled pillows. The refined detailing, the orderly arrangement of objects on
the mantel, and the absence of clutter in both the Inman reception room
and parlor signal the growing influence of eighteenth-century French
classicism on Atlanta interiors.

FACING PAGE: Fig. 2.9   RECEPTION ROOM, SAMUEL AND MILDRED INMAN RESIDENCE, 1897

[34] L. B. Wheeler, "Furniture," *Atlanta Constitution*, 10 January 1886, 8.

Dining Room. Within the hierarchy of the social house's ceremonial spaces, the dining room was without peer. As befitting its status and as the setting for the climax of the evening's entertainments, considerable time, money, and newspaper copy were spent on its decoration. Detailed descriptions of Atlanta dining rooms were the frequent focus of newspaper articles. In describing the dining room as "the glory of woman and bonhomie to man,"[35] one Atlanta writer affirmed the dining room's dual gender associations. From the correct setting of the table and quality of the tableware, to the preparation and service of the meal, the dining room was a showcase for the woman's ability to make a home. On the other hand, if the number of Atlanta photographs of all-male dinner parties is any indication, it is clear that the dining room was a man's space. Its dark paneled walls and massive, elaborately carved furniture suggested a strong male identity and spoke to a man's ability to provide for his family and to properly entertain guests. Encircled by gleaming woodwork, sitting in richly carved chairs at a table set with the finest in silver, crystal, and porcelain, and with plush carpets underfoot, guests ate in a convivial atmosphere, surrounded by the family's material bounty.

L. B. Wheeler's criteria for a well-designed dining room centered on adequate space for a guest's comfort and for servants to perform their duties at table. For instance, a hot fireplace should be at a comfortable distance from people seated at the table; and as it was the custom for men to escort ladies in a procession to the dining room, doors must be wide enough for the passage of "two abreast."[36]

If the effect of the parlor was froth and light, the desired effect of the dining room was substance. Dining room walls were heavily detailed. Wall surfaces above the paneled wainscoting were frequently covered with leather or materials such as embossed papers that produced a leather effect and could be painted and then bronzed.[37] Lincrusta Walton, a material similar to lightweight linoleum, was especially adaptable for use in dining rooms and other high-maintenance areas, such as halls, as it could be cleaned with a damp sponge. Dark, warm reds, Indian red, olive green, and browns highlighted by gilding were common hues in the somber palette of the 1880s. Fruit, especially grapes and pomegranates, bunches of wheat, and brightly plumed iridescent birds were reoccurring motifs. Equally popular, though hardly as appetizing, were images of dead game or fish

[35] "Beauty and Magnificence," *Atlanta Constitution,* 13 October 1889, 14.
[36] L. B. Wheeler, "Dining Rooms," *Atlanta Constitution,* 3 January 1886, 8.
[37] "Fashions in Furnishings," *Atlanta Constitution,* 7 October 1883, 4.

Fig. 2.11   DINING ROOM, SAMUEL AND MILDRED INMAN RESIDENCE, 1897

carved on sideboards or painted on walls—a gesture to the skills of the hunter[38] that had once been essential to survival and that were now relegated to sport.

Dark paneled walls and Renaissance Revival-style furniture give the Inman dining room, shown in figure 2.11, the necessary air of dignified masculinity. With its architectural quality, ample molding, and elaborately carved surfaces in mahogany, black walnut, or rosewood, the Renaissance Revival furniture exuded the baronial splendor that appealed to successful Atlanta commercial and financial leaders. The Inman chairs are upholstered in leather, a typical material chosen for its resistance to staining and embellishment options such as embossing and illuminating. Tapestry weaves were a common alternative. Lining chairs along the wall facilitated extending and setting the table. A built-in sideboard replaced the massive, freestanding variety that loomed over diners throughout much of the late nineteenth century. Still suitably carved and detailed to meet the need for ostentation and display, it also provided efficient storage for the copious amount of "things" required for dining in style. Large mirrors behind displays of china and silver amplified the available light as well as the visual

[38] Kenneth L. Ames, *Death in the Dining Room and Other Tales of Victorian Culture* (Philadelphia: Temple University Press, 1992) 73.

Fig. 2.12 DINING ROOM, HENRY AND NORA TOMPKINS RESIDENCE, 1897

impact of the owner's possessions. Fluted columns flank windows treated with lace curtains covered by outer drapery and swags bound by ropes and tassels. As in the reception and parlor, the ceiling is painted in a bordered pattern of floral swags.

Judge Henry B. Tompkins's dining room, seen in figure 2.12, is as ornate and highly theatrical as any found in Atlanta. Raised in the elegant surroundings of his boyhood home in Alabama, Judge Tompkins had a life-long appreciation for the finer things, which he spared no expense in securing for his new residence on Peachtree Street. The 45-foot dining room is covered with a vaulted ceiling painted in tints of old ivory to simulate relief carving. On either side of the entrance, built-in buffets are set in arched, frescoed alcoves. The color scheme of the room is a combination of dark, East Indian mahogany woodwork and shades of terra cotta found on upholstery, drapery, and walls. The floors are covered with imported Eastern rugs.[39] Mahogany Chippendale-style chairs surround an extension table supported on massive lion paws.

[39] Dooly, "Handsome Interiors," 6.

had been laid. However, by the end of the decade the city's 9,000 privies still vastly outnumbered the 2,829 water closets, and it was 1912 before Atlanta had its first sewage treatment plant.[46]

✦ *Nursery.* Like Atlantans' bedrooms, few of their nurseries were photographed before the turn of the century; however, images and descriptions of the nurseries of several lucky Atlanta children appeared in the 15 April 1906 *Atlanta Constitution.* As might be expected, nurseries contained small metal beds, lined up side by side, child-sized desks, tables, chairs, and chests. One photo captured children sitting on the floor, surrounded by toys, while their nursemaid stood watch in the background. It was a snapshot of a moment in the daily life of an upper-middle-class, white Southern child.

Considerable thought went into the decorative treatments on nursery walls. Scenes from popular children's literature and the work of important illustrators such as W. W. Denslow and Cecil Aldin provided thematic and artistic content for decorative friezes. In Master Henry Grady's nursery, a frieze painted with scenes from the Uncle Remus tales paid homage to the region's literary heritage and his grandfather's close friend Joel Chandler Harris, author of the Uncle Remus books.[47] Little Dorothy Arkwright, daughter of Mr. and Mrs. Preston Arkwright, had what the *Atlanta Constitution* described as a "William Morris" nursery, because it combined "simplicity with art and is an object lesson besides." For her enjoyment and edification, the walls contained a series of Cecil Aldin's illustrations depicting the complete story of Noah's ark and letters of the alphabet decorated a low chest.[48]

The objects in Dorothy's room also reflected an early lesson in gender typing. Her white painted furniture included a low dressing table with mirror, dolls, and a table set for tea. The "Japanese" and "Indian" corners were devoted to the development of her artistic skills and cultural awareness, reflections of her parents' aspirations for their progeny. Likewise, a room off Master Henry Grady's bedroom contained a miniature pool table where, Isma Dooly explained, "Master Grady and his guests may take their first lessons in one of the gentlemanly sports."[49]

FACING PAGE: *Fig. 2.14* BEDROOM, JOHN AND FANNY GORDON RESIDENCE, CA. 1895

---

[46] Franklin M. Garrett, *Atlanta and Environs: A Chronicle of Its People and Events, 1880s–1930s,* vol. 2 (Athens: University of Georgia Press, 1969) 209–10.
[47] Isma Dooly, "Many Beautiful Nurseries Nestle in the Homes of Atlantans Where Youngsters Hold Sway," *Atlanta Constitution Magazine,* 15 April 1906, 2.
[48] Isma Dooly and Cora Toombs, "Dorothy Arkwright's Nursery," *Atlanta Constitution,* 12 April 1903, 2, 4. In this article, the illustrator was referenced as Cecil Arden but almost certainly refers to Cecil Aldin.
[49] Dooly, "Many Beautiful Nurseries," 2.

BEHIND THE SCENES: THE DOMESTIC STAFF

Maintaining these huge houses required a sizable domestic staff. At the rear of the first floor were the kitchen, pantry, and butler's pantry, which, along with the lower-level laundry, storerooms, and refrigerator rooms, comprised the domain of the largely African-American domestic work force it took to sustain the life of the social house. Housemaids, cooks, laundry women, children's nursemaids, gardeners, butlers, and groomsmen worked long hours for low pay. They polished miles of ornate moldings, washed hundreds of windowpanes, beat Oriental rugs, lit coal fires, washed, starched, and ironed linen, and cooked and served meals for family and guests. A set of back stairs allowed servants to carry out their tasks discreetly with little inconvenience to the owners or their guests.

Living arrangements for servants varied by household. Some house workers, such as maids, cooks, and butlers, occupied rooms on the third floor of the main house, the attic, or separate accommodations behind the family home. Others, such as laundry women, preferred to live separately from their employers for a greater sense of independence.[50] In some households, the relationship between servants and the family was amiable, even familial. In figure 2.15, "Mammy McGruder" stands at her cast-iron stove and smiles indulgently at young Helen Turman. Though most likely posed, the image nonetheless reveals the mutual affection that existed between servants and their young charges. However, in other homes servants and owners existed in an unspoken yet clearly communicated tension created by generations of racial prejudice, resentment, and distrust.[51]

Though the Atlanta home continued to be influenced by deeply engrained regional attitudes regarding class and race, in the organization of the plan and hierarchy of household members, nineteenth-century Atlanta homes were a microcosm of the socially stratified Victorian era. Likewise, in the interior decoration of their homes, Atlantans strove to reshape their surroundings and lifestyles along more contemporary, national lines. Photographs offer proof that they succeeded; Atlanta interiors are indistinguishable from those in countless homes throughout the country.

In the pursuit of their domestic ideal, Atlantans were aided by the city's growing position as a transportation center that provided access to a pool of national manufacturers of interior furnishings. However, affluent Atlanta

---

[50] Georgina Hickey, *Hope and Danger in the New South City* (Athens: University of Georgia Press, 2003) 114.
[51] Ibid., 113.

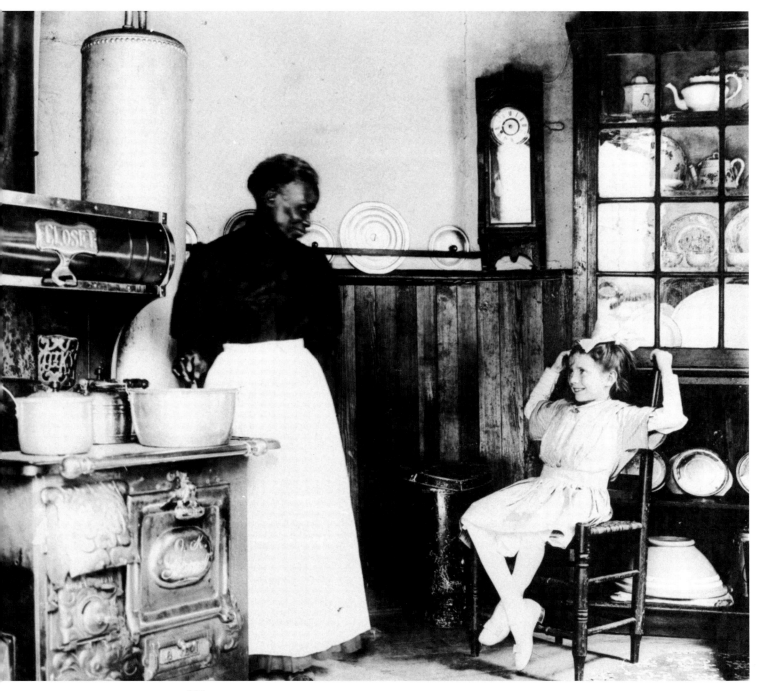

Fig. 2.15 "Old kitchen," Samuel and Helen Turman residence, ca. 1905

consumers who aspired to more distinctive surroundings needed more than access to goods. They required the services of architects, artists, and craftsmen to make their vision a reality. By the 1880s, retailers and professionals in all areas of interior decoration found wealthy Atlanta homeowners both willing and able to support a growing interiors market.

Atlanta buyers in search of home furnishings would likely begin their search on Whitehall Street, the heart of the city's retail district. All the important stores were located on Whitehall, anchored by the department stores M. Rich & Bros. (Rich's); Chamberlin, Boynton, and Company, later Chamberlin, Johnson, DuBose Co. (Chamberlin's); and J. M. High & Co. (High's). In addition to department stores, numerous small retailers specialized in home furnishings for the middle class, including two well-known Atlanta establishments, the A. G. Rhodes Furniture Company and the Haverty Furniture Company. In 1889, J. J. Haverty and Amos Rhodes became partners in the Rhodes-Haverty Furniture Company. With Amos Rhodes's development of the installment plan, he and other enterprising retailers made it possible for even the thriftiest buyer to join in the national fervor to consume.

Dry-goods stores, some of which had been among the earliest businesses to open following the Civil War, expanded their inventory to become the city's first department stores. The most successful of these retailers were Chamberlin's, opening in 1866, and a year later, Rich's. Both stores benefited from the economic boom of the 1880s, doing a highly competitive business in the area of carpet and drapery and offering the finest imported materials, rugs, and carpets from Europe and Asia. But in the realm of fine furniture, Chamberlin's enjoyed preeminent ranking among Atlanta's department stores.

Chamberlin's marketed to the discerning upper-class buyer or "carriage trade" and offered only the highest quality goods. Considerable advertising dollars were spent in the store's attempt to elevate public taste to the level of their high-end products. Their effusive newspaper advertisements were tutorials on what to look for in quality interior furnishings and the importance of permanence over the purchase of novelties. Chamberlin's copywriters even proffered their own definition of "good taste" to the growing number of opinions on the subject: "It is the mark of genuine good taste to know a good thing when it is out of style."[52] By the 1870s, Chamberlin's was the most successful retailer in the city. The 1879 view of Chamberlin's drapery and carpet departments, shown in figure 2.16,

---

[52] Chamberlin, Johnson, DuBose Co. advertisement, *Atlanta Journal*, 12 November 1897, 6.

illustrates the Atlanta homeowner's shopping experience of the late nineteenth century.

In 1885, Chamberlin's opened an elegant new five-story glass building. By 1889, the furniture department occupied a 190-by-50-foot space lit by electric lights. A writer for the *Atlanta Constitution* visiting the furniture hall in 1889 described goods merchandised in ways new to the South. Shoppers moved through well-organized displays of furnishings grouped by room: hall, library, office, dining room, bedroom, and parlor. Furthermore, furniture was displayed in such an organized way that no pieces were touching. The result was receipts that reached into "hundreds of thousands annually, and sales covering many of the Southern states."[53]

> "There is not a finer furniture house in all the country,
> and [Chamberlin's is] by far the largest south of Cincinnati."
> "Beauty and Magnificence," *Atlanta Constitution*, 13 October 1889

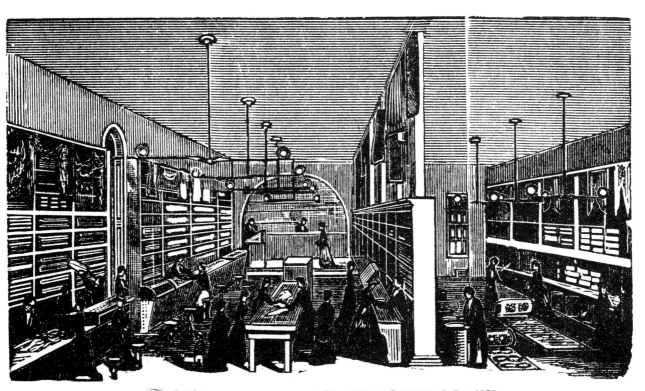

Fig. 2.16 Interior illustration, Chamberlin, Boynton & Co., 1879

[53] "Beauty and Magnificence," 14.

In 1887, Rich's added its South Annex to accommodate a complete furniture department, which grew into seven salesrooms by 1892.[54] With a reputation for customer service, quality merchandise, and a more inclusive target market, Rich's enjoyed the greatest longevity in Atlanta's retail history and remained an Atlanta institution for over 130 years.

Through their lavish display windows, innovative in-store merchandizing, and advertisements, department stores were the buyer's best local source of information on current furniture styles and interior treatments. For homeowners in need of more personalized guidance in their decorating decisions, department stores also offered the services of specialists such as furnishers and drapers. A "furnisher" was someone who provided window-treatment and upholstery services and selected furnishings. "Drapers" focused exclusively on the treatments for windows and other interior details in need of embellishment with soft goods. A 12 November 1897 advertisement in the *Atlanta Constitution* offers a description of the services provided by a Chamberlin's draper: "If you want to adorn a room with Draperies,

Fig. 2.17 Postcard of Whitehall Street sent 1914

[54] Richard Joel, "A Brief History of Rich's," *Atlanta Historical Bulletin,* 7/27 (January–April 1942): 8.

consult our artist. He will go to your home, survey the various arches, niches, alcoves, window recesses, and make pen-and-ink or water-color sketches of the hangings most appropriate…. He is a wizard."[55]

In the summer of 1898, Chamberlin's raised the bar in the merchandizing of home furnishings with the completion of their first model rooms: five rooms filled with furnishings suitable for both average and upscale interiors.[56] At this point, Chamberlin's led the field among Atlanta purveyors of home decoration. It was a position they would continue to strengthen and expand as the practice of interior decoration evolved in the early years of the coming century.

By the late nineteenth century, the section of Whitehall Street shown in figure 2.17 had become Atlanta's earliest center for home decoration. In 1885, Chamberlin's moved into their new building, the five-story, red brick building seen on the right. Rich's, Chamberlin's closest competitor, is seen in the next block. To the right of Chamberlin's is Lycett's studio, where Atlanta women perfected the feminine art of china painting.

NINETEENTH CENTURY TASTEMAKERS

Along with drapers, upholsterers, and furnishers, wealthy Atlantans had at their disposal the services of architects, interior decorators, artists, and cabinetmakers. Together, these professionals comprised the cadre of specialists required to create Atlanta's most fashionable interiors. They were also the city's ultimate authorities on what constituted good taste.

✦ *Architects.* Before the emergence of the professional interior decorator in the early twentieth century, stylistic decisions, interior details, and surface treatments were the purview of the architects, who acted as consultants to clients, advising them on selections or, in many cases, making all interior decoration decisions. They designed rugs, built-in and freestanding furniture, and collaborated with artists or interior decorators in the installation of murals and other custom interior finishes; in some instances, they designed the artwork themselves. The rendering by W. T. Downing in figure 2.18 is an example of the architect's concept for the decorative finishes of a late nineteenth-century Atlanta interior. Set against paneled walls and a

[55] Chamberlin, Johnson, DuBose Co. advertisement, *Atlanta Journal*, 12 November 1897, 6.
[56] "Chamberlin, Johnson, DuBose Co." *Atlanta Constitution*, 16 June 1898, 02.

plaster ceiling, the polychromatic color scheme of the frieze is carried throughout the space.

Though Atlanta architects frequently worked with local retailers such as Rich's and Chamberlin's in the purchase and installation of furnishings, their access to resources extended well beyond Whitehall Street. For the more discerning client, architects traveled to Chicago or New York in search of the finest in wallpapers and furnishings. In cases where local talent was unavailable, artisans and artists were imported from the North or even Europe to complete the exacting details. Atlanta architects Bruce and Morgan, L. B. Wheeler, and W. T. Downing worked through Chamberlin's to purchase furniture from the Cincinnati firm Robert Mitchell Furniture Co. For the home of Hugh T. Inman, architects Wheeler and Downing chose the studio of Pollmer, Tumoor and Mark, of Cincinnati and New York, to complete the home's frescos to harmonize with other interior treatments.[57]

 Interior Decorators. By the 1880s, craftsmen skilled in the arts of home decoration—furnishers, drapers, and interior decorators—had opened businesses in Atlanta. Their advertisements indicate that "interior decorator" was a term loosely applied to suppliers of a variety of services, but one which referred primarily to the treatment of interior surfaces for homes, hotels, retail stores, churches, and other public buildings. While many who carried the title "decorator" were probably little more than skilled paperhangers, others were artists in the true sense of the word. The scope of their services could include the design and painting of murals and frescos; the selection of elaborate combinations of papers for walls, ceilings, friezes, and dados; and finishes such as gilding, graining, glazing, and marbleizing. Other services included woodcarving, plaster casting, and the design of custom furnishings.

Among the most successful interior decoration firms to open in Atlanta in the 1880s was Pause, Schroeter & Co., whose advertisement is seen in figure 2.19. Oscar Pause's work included the 1883 renovation of the Governor's Mansion and the home of Livingston and Sue Mims. The description of his work for the Mims's dining room suggests that Pause, in addition to his expert technical skill, was fluent in the language of the rich

[57] "Fine Interiors," *The Southern Architect,* 1/5 (March 1890): 61.

Fig. 2.18 Interior rendering, W. T. Downing, architect

and unusual color combinations dominating high-end interiors of the 1880s:

> The dado is of gold and bronze in a rich, bas-relief fruit design of pome-
> granates and grapes. The walls are of Pompeiian red shading into dull blur
> overhead, and the freize [sic] with its dull red ground has bronze designs
> representing the heads of satyrs peeping from intertwined grape vines.
> The centerpiece, from the middle of which a beaten bronze chandelier is
> suspended, is a magnificent fresco in Egyptian blue and Pompeiian red
> arabesques.[58]

By the early 1880s, a few Atlanta interior decorators had begun to bridge the gap between interior decorating and furnishing. One of the earliest Atlanta firms to combine the services of furnishers, drapers, and fresco artists was that of E. S. Lathrop and his junior partner, J. T. White. In their store on Marietta Street, the decoration department's four vignettes allowed customers to view completed installations of an assortment of wallpaper, carpet, and drapery in the latest styles, colors, and combinations. Lathrop furnished a number of high-end homes in Atlanta and the South, developing a reputation in the city as an artist of impeccable taste. He

O. PAUSE.   A. SCHROETER.   F. A. FISCHER.

Pause, Schroeter & Co.
DECORATORS IN FRESCO,

——) FURNITURE, DRAPERY, (——

And all Interior Decorations, Private Residences, Churches, etc.

Stained Glass Manufacturers, and Agents for the George Mertz's Turned Mouldings.

Sketches for Fresco or Stained Glass made and forwarded free on application.

Branch: 1455 Broadway, New York,)   8 North Broad Street,
Next to Rossmore Hotel.)

ATLANTA, GA.

Fig. 2.19 ADVERTISEMENT, PAUSE, SCHROETER & CO., 1890

[58] "Atlanta Dining Rooms," *Atlanta Constitution*, 25 November 1888, 11.

selected everything for the interior, including furniture, paintings, carpet, and drapery, in addition to the decorative treatments for walls and ceilings. One of his contemporaries compared him to New York interior decorator and furniture manufacturer Leon Marcotte, who would "not even put down a carpet or hang a picture, unless it is his own selection."[59] In Atlanta, Lathrop became a transitional figure between the nineteenth-century artist/decorator and the professional interior decorator that would emerge in the early years of the twentieth century.

"Give me a house as it comes from the hands of the plasterer.
Let me select for it throughout every article of furniture,
carpeting, drapery, wall paper and whatever else is needed, and I
will guarantee an effect that will be pleasing and satisfactory."

E. S. Lathrop, *Atlanta Constitution*, 1 September 1881

Among the services professionals offered to clients, none was more vital to the success of the interior than guidance with decisions regarding style. Prevailing conditions within nineteenth-century furniture design and manufacturing made the selection of style a daunting undertaking for the uninitiated. Affluent buyers relied on professionals with their access to finely crafted, hand-finished pieces. The average buyer, however, was left adrift amid the dizzying array of styles and cheap, machine-produced furniture that dominated Whitehall Street.

[59] "Interior Decorations," *Atlanta Constitution*, 12 March 1882, 5.

Fig. II.1　Entry hall, William and Rebecca Sanders residence, 1897

INTERIORS OF WALTER T. DOWNING, ARCHITECT

Walter T. Downing was born in Boston and moved to Atlanta as a young boy. He began his architectural career as an apprentice in the firm of L. B. Wheeler, where his first work as an architect was to assist Wheeler on the rebuilding of the Kimball House Hotel. In 1890, Downing established his own firm, where, until his death in November 1918, he was the architect of choice of a number of Atlanta's wealthy and influential citizens. To be the owner of a "Downing home" became a status symbol among those who could afford to pay his fees.[60]

A record of his residential work was preserved through his book *Domestic Architecture*, published in 1897. The numerous interior photographs by F. L. Howe provide a rare compendium of upscale Atlanta interiors of the late nineteenth century. Descriptions of several of these homes and their interiors were featured in local newspaper articles that provide information on color, fabrics, and other details the photos do not reveal.

Though the extent of Downing's participation in the selection of interior furnishings and treatments is difficult to determine, images of his most fashionable homes share several similarities and suggest more than a passing amount of professional involvement. The interiors show a restraint found wanting in most nineteenth-century homes. There is order in the placement of furniture. Downing, like other nineteenth-century architects, used built-in furniture to streamline the plan and eliminated unnecessary pieces that crowded Victorian homes. Tables and mantels are uncluttered. His use of panels and surface treatments such as murals and frescos, gilding,

---

[60] "Walter T. Downing, Atlanta Architect, Died on Thursday," *Atlanta Constitution*, 2 November 1918, 8.

and scagliola, a technique for imitating marble, and marbleizing discouraged owners who might be tempted to "decorate" the interior as soon as the architect and his photographer were out of the door.

In many cases, furniture appears to have been selected and arranged for each individual space. Downing's interiors featured all the furniture styles current at the end of the century: reproductions of Early Georgian, Chippendale, the Italian Renaissance, the Louis Revivals, and the Empire. The use of more generic upholstered pieces, such as tufted chairs and sofas, met the need for comfort, if not style.

One of Downing's most stylistically unique interiors was that of successful cotton broker William C. Sanders and his wife, Rebecca Hulsey. For the Sanders home on desirable Washington Street, Downing brought his concept of Roman classicism into the interior detailing and finishes. Through consistent use of classical motifs, old ivory trims, and embroidered hangings in all arches and doorways, Downing achieved a more visually unified interior than those found in many of the city's social houses.

Fig. II.2   DINING ROOM, WILLIAM AND REBECCA SANDERS RESIDENCE, 1897

In the entry hall and dining room, Downing shows his enthusiasm for elaborate surface treatments. The wall finish of the Sanders entry hall, figure II.1, is scagliola,[61] an Italian method for imitating marble consisting of a mixture of plaster of Paris and marble chips. The tiger with his gaping mouth appears to be smiling as he greets visitors to the home and suggests either the photographer, architect, or owner had a sense of humor.

In the dining room, figure II.2, the walls are treated with carved panels painted in old ivory and gold. The tapestry pattern in the frieze is repeated in the chair cushions. For the portières, a tapestry fabric is used to face the dining room while soft, green velvet faces the entry hall. The furniture is mahogany. To the left, a buffet is built-in below two mosaic glass windows and flanked by a china closet said to be "filled with the most exquisite china, and Bohemian glass."[62] Silver sconces provide the room's illumination.

In the sitting room, figure II.3, simpler wall treatments allow the highly detailed frieze and cornice treatment to take center stage.

Compared to the Sanders residence, the interior of the Peachtree Street home Downing designed for Frank E. and Margaret Cochran Block is more

[61] Isma Dooly, "Features of Interest to Our Women," *Atlanta Constitution Magazine*, 26 November 1899, 7.
[62] Ibid.

Fig. II.3 SITTING ROOM, WILLIAM AND REBECCA SANDERS RESIDENCE, 1897

Fig. II.4   ENTRY HALL, FRANK AND MARGARET BLOCK RESIDENCE, 1897

reserved and stately. Two views of the hall, not found in Downing's book, illustrate the importance Victorian Atlantans placed on the first impression. The spacious main hallway, figure II.4, with its easel supporting framed artwork and the figure on a marble stand, give the room the feel of an art gallery. Its generous size accommodated the wedding of the Block's daughter Isabel to Brooks Morgan in 1902. With its highly veined marble and what was described as a "high cabinet mantel,"[63] the massive fireplace made a suitable altar before which the bride and groom took their vows. The furniture, seen in both views of the room, is part of an upscale suite.

To the right, past the sculpture, is the stairway with stained-glass windows seen in figure II.5. Tucked to the right of the stairs is a built-in bench, a familiar Downing detail. Here, one could read or listen to the

[63] "Wedding of Miss Block and Mr. Brooks Morgan," In the Social Realm, *Atlanta Constitution*, 20 March 1902, 9.

Fig. II.5   STAIRWAY, FRANK AND MARGARET BLOCK RESIDENCE, 1897

phonograph and be warmed by central heat. The settee appears to have been positioned for the photograph.

The Block parlor, figure II.6, is light and delicate in detailing. The intricately patterned lace curtains emit considerable light. The fireplace is detailed with white marble and graceful, slender columns rising to a bordered ceiling decorated with arabesques and flowers. A highly ornamented chandelier and equally as ornate, lightweight furniture contribute to the room's air of refinement.

More subdued than the parlor, the sitting room, figure II.7, has a less formal atmosphere. The fireplace detailing is heavier and the marble darker in value. The tufted leather chairs, smoking stand, and cuspidor would support the man of the house at his leisure.

Fig. II.6   PARLOR, FRANK AND MARGARET BLOCK RESIDENCE, 1897

Fig. II.7   SITTING ROOM, FRANK AND MARGARET BLOCK RESIDENCE, 1897

In figure 3.4, the walls above the wainscoting of Henry Grady's study are covered in a highly patterned, bordered wallpaper. The geometric patterns on the pillow and the textile lying on the sofa are Eastern in influence. The sofa has Eastlake detailing. A telephone, one of the first in an Atlanta home, is barely visible on the wall to the left.

A model of Aesthetic ideals, the parlor of the Jack D. Small family, figure 3.5, displays both artistic pretensions and individuality. The wallpaper, a small-scale, stylized leaf motif popular in the 1880s, serves as a backdrop for artwork and other decorative objects. An "art corner" has been arranged and consists of a landscape print on an easel, a small painted screen, and an autoharp. Eastlake-style frames are neatly arranged on the draped mantel along with several small pieces of pottery and items collected from nature. That the owner documented her efforts in a photograph indicates a pride in her work. It was a two-person job. Barely visible to the right is an aproned woman standing on a chair, to hold the picture in place above the mantel while someone takes the photograph.

Aesthetic sensibilities found their greatest expression in the craze for wallpaper and painted interior decoration that accompanied the elaborate Queen Anne architecture of the 1880s. Pattern dominated the interior as highly decorative treatments, including complex wallpaper combinations, murals, frescos, and plaster decoration, covered walls and ceilings of the homes of affluent Atlantans. Descriptions of color schemes convey a vivid image of the era's complex, often exotic combinations of values and hues, enlivened by iridescence and the burnished luster of gold, silver, and copper.

In an 1884 interview with the *Atlanta Constitution*, well-known Atlanta decorator Abram Frank, whose work was said to rival anything found in New York, commented on the interest in the "Art Aesthetic" among his Atlanta patrons: "There never was anything like it. Everybody has gone *crazy* over household decorations. People who, a few years ago, thought that the greatest beauty lay in the plainest white walls...are now [the] very best patrons for the most elegant wall paper [*sic*], with the most elaborate dados and friezes that money will buy." When asked what new patrons wanted in decoration, he replied, "To get the very finest; never stopping to consider the cost. My experience has been that those who never had decorations in their houses, and who have seen them elsewhere, never fail to want the best."[71]

[71] "The Art Aesthetic," *Atlanta Constitution*, 2 March 1884, 9.

The painting of murals or frescos on walls and ceilings remained a prominent feature in Atlanta homes well after the turn of the century. Their subject matter varied considerably, from more generic images of landscapes, vegetation, and floral borders and sprays to highly personalized statements of the owner's interests. While most were the work of professional artists or interior decorators, others were painted by women whose homes became their canvas, as women widened their involvement in the art of interior decoration.

L. B. Wheeler was architect to several wealthy Atlantans during the 1880s when the popularity of Aestheticism was at its height. Though his career in Atlanta spanned less than a decade, Wheeler's influence on interior decoration in the city was noteworthy enough to inspire a Henry Grady editorial praising an unidentified Atlanta interior that Grady predicted would revolutionize residential architecture in the city.[72] The Queen Anne-style house Wheeler and partner William H. Parkins designed for John and Adeline Dougherty Silvey is one likely candidate for that unnamed home.

Known later as the Silvey-Speer home, the house was built in 1885–1887 on the corner of Marietta and Spring Street. In 1903, the house was moved to 1223 Peachtree Road, where the Silvey's daughter Katie and her husband, William A. Speer, resided. John Silvey's home was expensively and elaborately detailed. It was built at a final cost of approximately $35,000, $6,000 of which was spent on the interior woodwork. Wheeler ordered the furniture, carpets, curtains, and decorations from Chicago and commissioned D. E. Livermore, a Chicago artist, to paint the frescos.[73] No photographs remain of the original interior; however, an 1888 description of the dining room illustrates Wheeler's Aesthetic sensibilities in the elaborate coloration and treatment of the walls of one of Atlanta's lost showplaces:

> Mrs. Silvey Has a Queen Anne Diningroom [sic] That is magnificent and perfect in every detail. The moquette carpet of dull blue and Pompeiian red, reflects the design above of irridescent [sic] blue with bronze arabesques. The high backed carved oak Queen Anne chairs are upholstered in brown Spanish leather, and the table is of old oak richly carved. The wainscoting is also of carved oak, the walls of irridescent [sic] blue

[72] "Death of Mr. L. B. Wheeler," *Atlanta Constitution*, 7 March 1899, 2.
[73] "Silvey's New Home," *Atlanta Constitution*, 13 March 1887, 11.

Fig. 3.5 PARLOR, JACK D. SMALL FAMILY RESIDENCE, 1889

Fig. 3.6 Entry hall, Frank and Mary Rice residence, ca. 1890

By the 1880s the antiques craze had reached Atlanta. Like revival styles, antiques suggested a heritage, old family, and old money. This was especially appealing to those whose family trees had shallow roots. By the end of the century, anything old had become a thing of beauty. The acquisition of fine antiques, either European or American, became a status symbol. For some society women, it seemed that the most important aspect of owning antiques was "to be known and envied for having the finest collection."[78]

> "The relic[s] of the war-wrecked south supply the market mostly, but these rich mines will be shut off as the old family pride comes back with their retrieved fortunes, and they begin again to attach some value to the relics of their former glory."
>
> "The Antique Still Wanted," *Atlanta Constitution*, 10 August 1885

New England was considered the mother lode for American colonial antiques; however, by 1885 Northern dealers were lamenting the scarcity of antiques in that region and beginning to look farther south. From the earliest years of the colonial period, wealthy Southern planters had imported fine American furniture from Philadelphia and Newport to support their elegant lifestyles. Following the Civil War, many Southerners were forced to sell family silver, furniture, and other valuables. As wealthy Southerners began to recoup their fortunes, many discarded fine old pieces in favor of new styles. Others gave away older pieces to servants, who later made substantial profit from selling them to dealers[79] as antique hunting in the South reached a zenith in the 1920s. Scouts trolled Southern barns, smokehouses, and attics, where elegant examples of Sheraton, Hepplewhite, and Chippendale-style furniture lay ripe for the picking.

Homes such as that of Margie Calhoun, granddaughter of South Carolina statesman John C. Calhoun, offered antique hunters a cache of inherited spoils to plunder. In figure 3.11, the tufted Louis XV or Rococo Revival-style of her entry-hall parlor suite was popular during the Civil War and early years of Reconstruction. One of a set of classical dining chairs sits in the doorway. When she sold her house in 1901, it was said to have contained many "historical relics"[80] from her family.

---

[78] "Women and Bric-a-Brac," Women and Society, *Atlanta Constitution*, 6 August 1898, 9.
[79] "The Antique Still Wanted," *Atlanta Constitution*, 10 August 1885, 1.

Fig. 3.11 ENTRY HALL, MARGIE CALHOUN RESIDENCE, 1901

Fig. 3.12 Parlor, Margie Calhoun residence, 1901

Fig. 3.18 DRAWING ROOM, JOHN B. AND FANNY GORDON RESIDENCE, CA. 1895

rise in the Kirkwood area. From its columned veranda it afforded vistas as far as Kennesaw Mountain to the west and Stone Mountain to the east. The twenty-room house underwent several additions, including one the year before it was destroyed by fire in June 1899.[83] After the fire, General Gordon rejected suggestions that he build a home in the newer styles, saying "he wanted to see once more, and live within its walls, the dear old home which had been so long occupied by the Gordon family."[84] In 1904, Sutherland was selected as the model for the Georgia building at the Louisiana Purchase Exposition of the same year. In citing the house's qualifications for such an honor, W. G. Cooper, secretary of the Atlanta Chamber of Commerce, claimed that it represented the "good taste and refinement of our people…[while General Gordon] typifies the exalted character which men call southern chivalry."[85]

In General Gordon's drawing room, figure 3.18, a Rococo étagère, Turkish chairs, and Eastern-style rugs mix with relics of General Gordon's Confederate past. Barely visible on the left is a vignette that has the feeling

[83] "Gen. Gordon's House Burned," *Atlanta Constitution*, 22 June 1899, 5.
[84] "Around Gordon's Favorite Bench and 'Sutherland,' Memories Cling," *Atlanta Constitution*, 12 January 1904, 5.
[85] "May Reproduce Gordon's Home," *Atlanta Constitution*, 11 January 1904, 7.

Fig. 3.19 "Rise and Fall of the Confederacy," Amos and Amanda Rhodes residence

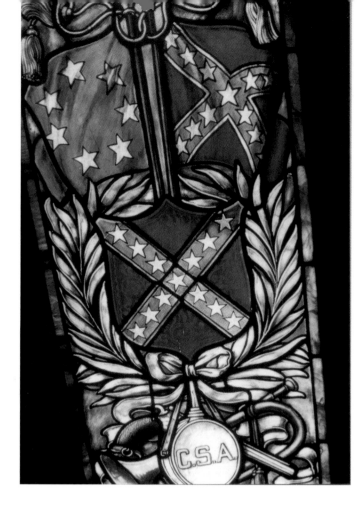

of a shrine: an armored knight on a pedestal stands sentinel before a Confederate flag-draped portrait of General Gordon. Another Confederate flag, identifiable by its white star, is placed to the right of the doorway.

A compelling example of the "Lost Cause" as reflected in an interior is found in the painted glass window above the entry hall staircase of the Amos and Amanda Dougherty Rhodes mansion, Le Rêve, figure 3.19. The window is a visual narrative of the rise and fall of the Confederacy. Beginning with the firing on Ft. Sumter, it chronicles battle scenes and likenesses of major Confederate leaders. It ends with a soldier returning to his ruined antebellum home, a poignant reminder of the cost of war. It is one man's memorial to the Confederacy, and perhaps a cautionary tale.

A footnote to the narrative appears in a small closet beneath the curving staircase, where images of Confederate flags are rendered in painted glass (figure 3.20). Its location invites interpretation: perhaps it is a silent statement of defiance or a private shrine. Or maybe, as it has been suggested, Rhodes, like other former Confederates who had made peace with the past, realized the time had come to put the flag away.

Fig. III.1   ENTRY HALL, WILLIAM AND MARY RAOUL RESIDENCE, CA. 1900

Fig. III.2   LIBRARY, WILLIAM AND MARY RAOUL RESIDENCE, CA. 1900

from a pole by small rings. The frayed mid-Eastern rug and stair carpet over worn wood floors add a romantic if somewhat shabby aura of age.

Visible beyond the stair landing is Captain Raoul's study, the walls of which were finished in a combed plaster technique that created a checkerboard effect.[95] For years, Captain Raoul displayed a bronze death mask of Napoleon on the desk in his study. It was one of three made by Napoleon's attending physician on St. Helena and had been presented to the city of New Orleans. Hidden during the siege of New Orleans, the mask was later uncovered by a member of the Raoul family. Prior to his death, Captain Raoul returned the mask to the city of New Orleans. Perhaps this was due in part to pressure from his wife, who, after looking at it for years, had packed it away in a linen closet.[96]

The library furniture in figure III.2, is a more typical eclectic mix of furniture: a Morris chair, flanked by a Turkish coffee table to its right, and to its left, a tea table. The shallow, drop-front desk to the right of the bookcase is similar to Gustav Stickley's "Chalet Desk."

HOUSE
PROUD

[95] Ibid., 131.
[96] Humphreys, "Never a 'Spider-Web' Party," 5.

Revelations of corruption and inefficiency in both government and business called into question the social values of the Victorian era, which were seen as having been driven by the relentless pursuit of profit and unbridled greed. Sensing the vulnerability of the Victorian ethos, critics began to circle. A new breed of journalists, social reformers, and progressive politicians took aim at a range of issues: women's suffrage, education, and public health, immorality, vice, and germs. Their efforts set America on a course of change in many areas of national life, including the nineteenth-century's ultimate expression of private wealth and class distinction, the home.

For decades, nineteenth-century critics had decried the declining conditions within the home. In Atlanta, L. B. Wheeler's criticisms of design in the mid-1880s were laced with reform sentiments. But Wheeler's wry comments on the aesthetic poverty of the wealthy were a far cry from the more strident voices of early twentieth-century reformers, whose rhetoric regarding the "redemption" and "salvation" of the home imbued their cause with religious fervor.

The issues of home reform were broad in scope, ranging from home sanitation, spurred by mounting fears over public health and the spread of communicable diseases, to the nineteenth-century obsession with the consumption and display of wealth. Caught in reformers' crosshairs were eclecticism and excess, which had resulted in garishly colored, highly patterned rooms, cluttered with what domestic science expert Lillian H. Johnston described as "dust accumulating, germ-bearing appurtenances" that made "museums out of the household."[100]

The artful display of goods seen in the Jack Small parlor (figure 4.2), once considered proof of artistic sophistication, became confirmation of its absence. Obtrusive wealth and possessions, once considered reliable indicators of one's moral worth, had now become idols with clay feet. Based on the belief that the new American home should support, not define, the life lived within its walls, the focus of home shifted from the presentation of a public face to the support of private family life. Such a home was understood now to be more than a matter of taste; it was also seen to be a valid concern of science.

[100] Lillian H. Johnston, "Modern Household Conveniences," *Atlanta Constitution*, 11 August 1912, G6.

Fig. 4.12 DINING ROOM, SAMUEL AND HELEN TURMAN RESIDENCE, CA. 1915

he built a family home to be shared by his sister Elizabeth Venable Mason, her husband, Frank T. Mason, and their children. From its materials to its interior decoration, his home paid homage to its locale as well as the Venable family lineage, interests, and livelihood. It was built of granite quarried from Stone Mountain, which was owned by Sam and his brother William. Venable family symbols, motto, and crest were incorporated into the detailing of several rooms. In the family living room, murals of scenes from the landscape around Mount Rest, the Venable retreat at Stone

Fig. 4.13 Dining room, Samuel and Helen Turman residence, ca. 1915

Mountain, were painted by his sister Leila Venable Ellis and T. S. Webster.[120] The "Oriental room," was filled with Chinese furniture and decorative arts. On the walls above the wainscoting, murals of exotic, mythological birds were painted on grass cloth. Among them, a painting of a phoenix enhanced with real peacock feathers gestured to the home's Atlanta context. [121]

From floor to ceiling, the house brims with intricate details. In the rendering of the two-story great hall, seen in figure 4.14, a leaded glass window rises the two-story height of the room. The walls are wrapped in oak wainscoting. The plaster ceiling is intricately molded and supported by beams that still bear the evidence of their green, gold, and red stenciling. On the east end of the room, the hooded stone fireplace carries the Venable coat of arms. The result is a room worthy of Sir Walter Scott.

Historical precedent remained a constant theme in the interiors of Atlanta homes, resisting any serious competition by Modernism or Art Deco in the years between the world wars and beyond. By 1920, driving

along the roads of Atlanta's new residential suburbs was a lesson in the history of European and American domestic architecture. The enduring appeal of the past testified to the importance accorded to memory and tradition in shaping Atlanta's domestic environment. It was a coming of age for Atlanta homes, their interiors, and the professionals who helped translate the new aesthetic into a reality: the professional interior decorator.

Fig. 4.14

THE GREAT HALL,
SAM VENABLE RESIDENCE,
STONEHENGE, 1913

[120] "Miss Leila Venable Mason Makes Debut at Stonehenge," *Atlanta Constitution*, 9 November 1929, 17.
[121] "Building Tour: A Tour of Stonehenge Mansion and the Sanctuary of St. John's Lutheran Church Atlanta, Georgia," n.p. Pamphlet prepared by St. John's Lutheran Church, Atlanta.

A TOUR OF
ATLANTA HOMES

RICHARD AND MARY JANE THOMPSON PETERS RESIDENCE

PEACHTREE STREET, 1881

Richard Peters grew up in Philadelphia, a member of a prominent Northern family. During an apprenticeship in the Philadelphia office of architect/engineer William Strickland, young Richard realized his gift for engineering. His work on the Georgia railroad as a civil engineer brought him to Atlanta in 1846. In 1848, he married Mary Jane Thompson, daughter of Atlanta pioneer Dr. Joseph Thompson. In addition to railroad building, Peters was involved in several other civic initiatives that contributed to Atlanta's postwar growth, including the move of the Georgia state capitol from Milledgeville to Atlanta and development of Atlanta's first streetcar company, the Atlanta Street Railway Company.[146] In 1881, Richard and his wife, Mary, built a stately new residence on Peachtree Street between 4th and 5th streets.

The embossed material filling the dado on the stair wall, seen in figure T.1, was probably Lincrusta Walton or Anaglypta, popular finishes for high-maintenance areas such as halls and dining rooms. The two folding chairs beneath the stairs are early models of today's "director's" chair. In the parlor, figure T.2, drapery hangs from rods, and a painted, translucent shade occupies the lower half of the window. The fireplace with its mirror and ample shelving has been dressed in assorted artful objects. A draped center table sits beneath a lighting fixture with an interesting detail. In the middle of the fixture is a large globe that could be lowered separately when a reading light was necessary.

---

[146] Thomas Martin, *Atlanta and Its Builders: A Comprehensive History of the Gate City of the South*, vol. 2 (Atlanta: Century Memorial Publishing Co., 1902) 688–90.

HOUSE
PROUD

HOUSE
PROUD

145

HOUSE
PROUD

Fig. T.2   PARLOR. RICHARD AND MARY PETERS RESIDENCE. 1880S

HOUSE
PROUD

147

HENRY AND SALLIE COBB JACKSON RESIDENCE

MITCHELL STREET, PRIOR TO 1864

enry Jackson was born in Savannah in 1845, the son of Henry R. Jackson, a U.S. diplomat and later a general in the Confederate army. His father was a cultured, scholarly man, a historian, and a poet. During the years his father served as Minister to Austria, young Henry received all the benefits of European travel and study in London and Vienna. After serving in the Civil War, Henry attended law school in Athens, Georgia, and came to Atlanta to practice. In 1867, he married Sallie Addison Cobb.[147]

In 1877, the Jacksons bought their home from Susan Solomon, widow of the home's builder, William Solomon. The house's proximity to the state capitol building made it convenient for use as the post headquarters of the Union army in 1864. In the early 1880s, the house underwent a major renovation, beginning with a veneer of Indiana limestone over the original red brick and a new front door and entry hall. A large window was added on the stair landing, and two rooms and a bath were built on the rear of the home. The doors between the double parlors were removed and replaced with columns,[148] as shown in figure T.3. The more open configuration resulting from the 1880s renovation was ideal for entertaining. In 1895, the parlor held 175 guests who witnessed the marriage of the Jacksons' daughter Cornelia to Wilmer L. Moore.[149] The Jacksons' draped piano functioned as an additional mantel for the display of photos and other bric-a-brac. The floor-length pier glasses between the far windows would have augmented the light and given the ladies and gentlemen ample opportunities to preen.

The newly enlarged dining room is seen in figure T.4. The room is clad floor to ceiling in dark, English oak. On the fireplace wall, an odd little niche occupies the space between the built-in sideboard to the left and fireplace to the right. With the dining table closed and armchairs facing the fireplace, the room is set for more informal, everyday use.

[147] Ibid., 666–67.
[148] Cornelia Jackson Moore, Moore Collection Moo-1, Kenan Research Center at the Atlanta History Center.
[149] "Moore-Jackson," *Atlanta Constitution*, 24 April 1895, 8.

Fig. T.3 Double parlor, Henry and Sallie Jackson residence, ca. 1890

Fig. T.4   DINING ROOM, HENRY AND SALLIE JACKSON RESIDENCE, CA. 1890

Fig. T.5   PARLOR, JOHN T. AND MARTHA GRANT RESIDENCE, CA. 1898

Fig. T.6   Vestibule, John W. and Annie Grant residence, 1897

JOHN W. AND ANNIE INMAN GRANT'S
FIRST RESIDENCE

PEACHTREE STREET, 1894

John W. Grant Sr. was a successful banker and land developer who, along with his father William, helped reshape the city's downtown business landscape. Two powerful Atlanta families were joined in 1893, when John married Annie Martin Inman, daughter of wealthy Atlanta businessman, Hugh T. Inman.[154]

W. T. Downing designed two homes for John and Annie Grant. The first house, built while the couple was on their year-long honeymoon in Europe, occupied a portion of the Peachtree Street property originally surrounding John's grandparents' mansion. John and Annie Grant lived in the house from its completion in 1894 until 1916, when they moved to their second home, Craigellachie.

In the Grants, Downing had a luxury most architects would have envied—clients whose taste matched their income. The result of their collaborations were two of the best examples of Atlanta high-style interiors of their day: the Peachtree home, exuberant, extravagant, and conspicuous; and Craigellachie, still grand, but with greater historical accuracy and congruity between the architecture, the interior detailing, and the furnishings.

In the small vestibule of their Peachtree Street home (figure T.6), a coatrack and umbrella stand store hats, coats, umbrellas, and canes, items necessary to make the transition from inside to outdoors. But this utilitarian space, with its serviceable brick tile floor, is not without an artistic component. The vaulted ceiling is decorated in delicate, Italian Renaissance arabesques that are repeated on the ceiling and frieze of the entry hall.

The massive marble slab, seen framing the fireplace on the back wall to the right, provides a dramatic focal point for the entrance hall (figure T.7). Softening the more architectural quality of the space, the pillows covering the built-in seating at the foot of the stairs and beneath the stained-glass window create the impression of a home that is both suitably dignified and comfortable.

---

[154] "John W. Grant Sr. Dies; Builder of Atlanta Skyline," *Atlanta Constitution*, 9 March 1938, 1.

Fig. T.7   ENTRY HALL, JOHN W. AND ANNIE GRANT RESIDENCE, 1897

Although the photograph in figure T.8 is labeled "parlor" in the table of contents of Downing's *Domestic Architecture*, this intimately scaled oval room is clearly the reception room, as indicated on the plan. Its exuberant French Rococo detailing makes this room truly one of a kind in Atlanta. Nowhere would the effect of walking in from a subdued, masculine entry into a light, feminine space be more striking than in the Grant home.

Fig. T.8 RECEPTION ROOM, JOHN W. AND ANNIE GRANT RESIDENCE, 1897

Fig. T.9   DINING ROOM, JOHN W. AND ANNIE GRANT RESIDENCE, 1897

Fig. T.10   DEN, JOHN W. AND ANNIE GRANT RESIDENCE, 1897

Cupids and clouds are painted on the ceiling. All walls, woodwork, and furniture are finished in tints of old ivory. The drapery is silvery green velvet. The furniture is upholstered in pastel green and rose silk, which also fills the wall panels flanking the doorway into the hall. The mirror over the mantel reflects a pictorial tapestry on the opposite wall set in an identically carved frame.[155]

By the early 1890s, old ivory woodwork had begun to replace the dark paneled dining room walls of the previous decades. Though not visible in the dining room photo (figure T.9), a paneled dado was said to contain a tapestry pattern that matched the upholstery on the chairs. The columned

[155] Isma Dooly, "Features of Interest to Our Women," *Atlanta Constitution Magazine*, 26 November 1899, 7.

opening leads to a small alcove filled with tropical plants.[156] A decorated ceiling completes the composition.

Tiles described as "Moroccan" are the focal point of Mr. Grant's otherwise plainly detailed den (figure T.10). A Renaissance Revival table, set at an angle to make best use of light, serves as a desk. A beer stein on the mantel and large leather chair with a cuspidor within spitting distance mark this room as a man's space.

[156] Ibid.

ALFRED HOLT AND SARAH BUNN COLQUITT RESIDENCE

MORELAND AND EUCLID AVENUE, 1884

The son of a U.S. senator and graduate of Princeton, Alfred Colquitt was a lifelong politician, serving Georgia in a variety of capacities including governor and as a U.S. congressman and senator.[157] In 1856, he married Sarah Bunn of Twiggs County, Georgia. The interior of the Colquitt's Edgewood-area home is an eclectic mix of late nineteenth-century styles and materials that were assembled over time. It is neither pretentious nor especially fashionable. The simplicity of its wall finishes was typical of homes of many affluent, upper-middle-class Atlantans for whom fashion wasn't a primary concern. Its simplicity may also have been an extension of what his friend Judge Richard H. Clark called Colquitt's "aversion to ostentation,"[158] an attitude shared by other Southerners of the Old Guard, who looked at the trend in new homes with the disdain normally reserved for the taste of Yankee industrialists. The interior photographs reflect the home of an older couple whose years of social activity were over. In 1892, Sarah suffered a stroke that left her partially paralyzed. Two years later, Senator Colquitt died. Sarah occupied the home until her death in 1898.

One interesting technological feature of the house was the use of Welsbach burners for lighting. Also referred to as a "gas mantle," this incandescent lighting produced an intense white light within a glass chimney. A white glass shade directed the light downward. The gas mantle competed with the new electricity until around 1910, when improvements to electric service rendered it obsolete.[159]

Opening to the rear of the entry hall is a spacious stair hall (figure T.11). The second-floor balustrade is barely visible at the top of the photo. The plain walls, lightweight furniture, and uncarpeted floors contribute to a sense of openness. The furniture is a typical late nineteenth-century Atlanta combination of Louis XV Revival and wicker, scattered round the room. Notice how the lighting has been placed across the door opening to the left of the square piano.

---

[157] Martin, 647. *Atlanta and Its Builders*.

[158] Richard H. Clark, "The Two Colquitts," *Atlanta Constitution*, 29 April 1894, 9.

[159] Denys Peter Myers, *Gaslighting in America: A Guide for Historic Preservation* (Washington DC: Office of Archeology and Historic Preservation, Heritage Conservation and Recreation Service, U.S. Dept. of the Interior, Technical Preservation Services Division, 1978) 207.

Fig. T.11 STAIR HALL, ALFRED AND SARAH COLQUITT RESIDENCE, CA. 1900

HOUSE
PROUD

Fig. T.12   Sitting room, Alfred and Sarah Colquitt residence, ca. 1900

167

The sitting room (figure T.12) has all the individuality and eclecticism of its day, without the more complex wall treatments. A small lady's writing desk and French chair are placed between two windows, while the table at the opposite window is set for tea. Photographs, books, and figurines have been grouped on the French-inspired center table. The chandelier has been modified to house a Welsbach burner.

The Colquitts' dining room (figure T.13) bears little resemblance to the ceremonial spaces found in Atlanta's more social homes. The walls are papered to resemble simple panels. Light streams in through lace curtains. The buffet on the back wall is Colonial Revival. The upholstered chair by the fireplace is a variation of the popular "Morris" chair. Though the table is laid with china and crystal, the typical set of dining chairs is nowhere to be found.

Fig. T.13   DINING ROOM, ALFRED AND SARAH COLQUITT RESIDENCE, CA. 1900

AMOS G. AND AMANDA DOUGHERTY
RHODES RESIDENCE, LE RÊVE

PEACHTREE STREET, 1904

Amos Giles Rhodes was born in Kentucky in 1850, the son of a wagonmaker. He came to Atlanta in 1875 and, a year later, married Amanda Dougherty of Marietta. In 1879 Amos formed the A. G. Rhodes Furniture Company and later became a partner in the Rhodes-Haverty Furniture Company. Though neither Amos nor Amanda came from privileged backgrounds, selling medium-priced furniture on the installment plan earned the Rhodeses a place among Atlanta's wealthiest families.

On a trip down the Rhine River in 1890, Amos and Amanda were said to have seen a castle that became the inspiration for their grand Romanesque Revival residence, Le Rêve. Designed by architect Willis Franklin Denny II and completed in 1904, the three-bedroom house was built as the Rhodeses' retirement home. With its massive, granite façade and crenellated turret, a billiard room, smoking room, and a den decorated in an American Indian theme, the home was largely a reflection of Amos's interests and tastes. If, with the exception of the hand-carved stairway, Rhodes used stock moldings and other cost-saving finishes throughout the house, he spared no expense when it came to the latest in home technology. A 1903 article in the *Atlanta Journal* reported that the house contained "burglar alarms, speaking tubes, call bells, house phones, central heat, and waterworks…" for its three and a half bathrooms. It was also fitted for both gas and electricity and contained more than 300 light bulbs.[160]

The photographs of the interior were done by the architect for his portfolio. However, he would have little opportunity to use them. In the winter of 1905, Denny caught pneumonia from which he never recovered. He died in August at the age of 31, a year after Le Rêve was completed.

The mahogany detailing in the reception hall (figure T.14) is in the Italian Renaissance style. Within each panel of the coffered ceiling, electric lights are set against a burnished gold background. When lit, they cast a mellow glow across the room. Above the paneling are frescos of the

---

[160] "Palatial New Residences Which Adorn Beautiful Peachtree Street," Feature Color Section, *Atlanta Journal*, 25 January 1903, 1.

Fig. T.14   RECEPTION HALL. AMOS AND AMANDA RHODES RESIDENCE. 1904

southern coastline. A full-length mirror covers the wall between the openings to the right. The Oriental rugs here and throughout the house were supplied by Joseph Wild and Co., New York.[161] Located above a curved stairway, the entry hall's focal point is a series of painted glass windows (figure 3.19, pgs. 90 and 91) depicting the rise and fall of the Confederacy. The intricately hand-carved, mahogany stairway is an Atlanta tour de force. Its newel-post is in the form of a menacing lion that looks to be standing guard over access to the second floor.

[161] Tommy Hart Jones, with Suber, Barber, Choate & Hertlein Architects, Inc. *Rhodes Memorial Hall: Historical Structure Report, Part One: History.* Prepared for the Georgia Trust for Historic Preservation, January 1998, 68–69.

Fig. T.15   Parlor, Amos and Amanda Rhodes residence, 1904

Though Amanda has been described as a deeply religious woman who preferred church work to society, her Louis XV parlor (figure T.15) was nonetheless fashionably detailed. The floral motifs and delicate arabesques painted on the ceiling and in the transoms are in pale tints of pink, green, and blue. The design of the parlor frescos and those on the dining room walls and library ceiling are thought to have been inspired by Willis Denny. The artist is unknown.[162] Old ivory woodwork frames walls hung in rose brocade which matched the upholstery fabric[163] on the gold leaf, Louis XV furniture still on order when the photograph was taken. In a 1930 *Atlanta Journal* article, Medora Perkerson described the portières as rose plush appliquéd over real lace.

[162] Ibid.
[163] "A Brilliant Reception at Beautiful 'Le Reve,'" Society, *Atlanta Constitution*, 13 November 1907, 8.

Fig. T.16 DINING ROOM, AMOS AND AMANDA RHODES RESIDENCE, 1904

The dining room's interior trim is golden oak (figure T.16). Walls covered in bronze-tinted leather[164] are topped by a frieze containing paintings of fish, fowl, and assorted fruits and vegetables. Wine-colored, plush velvet portières hang at the doorways. The brass and amber glass chandelier is suspended from a burnished bronze ceiling. Mirror-backed closets with glass doors displayed glass and china. Walls of the sliver closet were covered in a blue textile to reduce tarnishing. Built on the opposite end of the room are two Craftsman-style console tables and a sideboard over which a stained-glass window featuring a peacock was originally located.[165] The highly carved, golden oak furniture is in the Renaissance Revival style.

164 Ibid.
165 D.A. Crane, D.B. Payne and W.D. Heasley, "Architecture in Atlanta 1900–1919," chapter in *Atlanta Architecture*. A survey by students of the School of Architecture, Georgia Institute of Technology, Atlanta, 1949, 35.

Fig. T.17 Library, Amos and Amanda Rhodes residence, 1904

Though the room is referred to as the "library" in the 1904 image (figure T.17), seating lines the walls rather than built-in bookcases. The walls are covered with deep green damask above a mahogany dado, and the portières in green tapestry are trimmed with leather and metallic appliqué. Combined with the massive tufted leather chair and daybed and the presence of a cuspidor, the room conveys all the obligatory masculine associations of a library. However, a pale blue sky and symbols in three corners representing art, music, and literature painted on the ceiling in tints of blue, green, and pink suggest a more cultured female presence.

Fig. T.18   Den, Amos and Amanda Rhodes residence, 1904

Located on the front of the house is the den (figure T.18) where tradition says Amos Rhodes enjoyed watching the activity on Peachtree Street. The room's designation as the "Indian" room comes from the American Indian scenes painted on the coved ceiling and the artifacts decorating the room. Deep red walls, oak woodwork, and stenciled leather portières[166] complete the highly personalized decoration of this intimate space.

[166] Medora Field Perkerson, "Treasures in New Museum," *Atlanta Journal Magazine*, 18 May 1930, 3.

JOHN E. AND JULIA GATINS MURPHY RESIDENCE, HILLCREST

PEACHTREE STREET, 1905

ative Atlantan John E. Murphy was a prominent figure in the city's financial community and served on the board of a number of Atlanta companies. In 1893, he married Julia Gatins, daughter of Atlanta entrepreneur Joseph Gatins. In 1906, they moved into their new home, Hillcrest, built on a gentle rise at the northeast corner of Peachtree and 14th Street. The Murphys' notable hospitality and their home's sumptuous interior made an invitation to Hillcrest among the most coveted in Atlanta.

The Murphys were avid photographers. Their family album is a visual chronicle of the private life of a wealthy Atlanta family in the first half of the twentieth century. The images captured family members as they aged, married, and adapted to the rapid transformation of modern American life: children in pony carts, on horses, and later in cars; the Murphys traveling aboard ships and then airplanes; women in Victorian dress, in an array of costumes and gowns for social fetes, in Red Cross uniforms during World War I, and finally, women in pants.

To view the photographs of their home is to be invited into one of Atlanta's most social houses and the setting of some of the most lavish entertainments enjoyed by the city's upper crust. The Murphys' annual Christmas party was one of the most anticipated events of the Atlanta social season. Descriptions of its highlights have become part of Atlanta's social lore. Guests arrived promptly at eight o'clock and danced in the elegantly decorated ballroom until morning, when a light breakfast signaled the end of the festivities.[167]

Beginning in 1910 and continuing with few exceptions until 1986, opera parties were among Atlanta's most fashionable social affairs. The Murphys were ardent supporters of opera and helped to secure Atlanta's place on the Metropolitan Opera Company's yearly schedule. With her husband as a director of the Music Festival Association, Julia Murphy was one of the official hostesses of the organization. In entertaining the opera company's cast at dinners and parties during their spring visits to Atlanta,

---

[167] "Home of Mr. and Mrs. John E. Murphy," *Atlanta Journal Magazine*, 11 November 1923, 15.

Fig. T.19 ENTRY HALL, JOHN AND JULIA MURPHY RESIDENCE, CA. 1905

Julia became personal friends with several of the company's internationally known stars, including Antonio Scotti and Geraldine Farrar. Scotti, Farrar, Enrico Caruso, and others gave impromptu performances in the Murphy's magnificent ballroom, performing, as Julia explained, "as our friends, volunteering with gracious simplicity the music which we should have hesitated to ask for."[168]

Built at an estimated cost of $50,000,[169] the home conveyed in every detail the image of culture, luxury, and affluence. The detailing at Hillcrest was created by "Italian artisans who spent eighteen months carving and painting the interior walls and ceilings…"[170] Inlaid floors throughout the house were covered with handmade Austrian rugs. The photos of the home preserve a record of the good life lived in the final days of the Victorian age.

The entry hall (figure T.19), with its carved frieze and ceiling and crystal chandelier, creates an opulent first impression. The hall's paneled walls are hung with dark red velvet on which the Murphy monogram is emblazoned in gold threads. The richly carved mahogany furniture was described as Louis XV Revival. The draperies and portières have been removed, suggesting the photo was taken in the summer.

[168] Louise Dooly, "World Celebrities of Opera as Atlanta Woman Sees Them," *Atlanta Constitution*, 4 June 1913, 10A.
[169] "Many Homes are Building Throughout North Side," *Atlanta Constitution*, 25 March 1906, 8B.
[170] William B. Williford, *Peachtree Street, Atlanta* (Athens: University of Georgia Press, 1962) 99.

[171] Isma Dooly, "Beautiful Home of Mr. and Mrs. John E. Murphy," Atlanta's Social Realm, *Atlanta Constitution*, 23 December 1906, C2.

[172] "Home of Mr. and Mrs. John E. Murphy," 15.

When the interior was completed in 1906, Isma Dooly described the home's decoration in an article for the *Atlanta Constitution*. The woodwork and ceiling of the salon (figure T.20) were painted French gray and highlighted with gold leaf to match the gilded Louis XV furniture. Pale rose brocade satin was used on the walls, upholstery, and draperies.[171] A 1923 article in the *Atlanta Journal* described the drapery as soft rose velvet embroidered with gold by nuns in a French convent.[172] An event such as the 1922 wedding of the Murphy's daughter Julia in the salon would have provided a perfect excuse to replace dated hangings.

The walls of the French Renaissance-inspired dining room (figure T.21) are finished with highly polished mahogany paneling and tapestries of eighteenth-century pastoral scenes in greens and mahogany browns.

Fig. T.20 Louis XV salon, John and Julia Murphy residence, ca. 1905

Fig. T.21 Dining room, John and Julia Murphy residence, ca. 1905

The "hand-wrought, illuminated leather portières"[173] that hung in the doorway have been removed. The carved mahogany furniture includes a sideboard, extension table, and chairs upholstered in a tapestry weave. An opaque screen covers the fireplace opening, and a three-panel screen, decorated with a plumed peacock on a tree branch, is located to the right of the fireplace. The ceiling medallion was hand carved. Silk drapery, not seen in the photograph, hung over the lace curtains. Centered in the window to the right is a bronze figure referred to as the "Spirit of the Vineyard." Draped with clusters of glass grapes fitted with light bulbs,[174] it exemplifies the waning aesthetic of the late nineteenth century.

179

[173] Dooly, "Beautiful Home," C2.
[174] "Home of Mr. and Mrs. John E. Murphy," 15.

The breakfast room (figure T.22) is decorated with old ivory and gold trim and walls of Empire green. The wall covering on the dado is an embossed, fleur-de-lis pattern. An ivory and green glass chandelier hangs over the table.[175] Wires running from the sconces power the lights on the mantel and the electric fan. As late Victorian homes made the transition from gas to electricity, exposed wires would have been considered a minor nuisance compared to the advantages of electric light and a cool breeze.

[175] Dooly, "Beautiful Home," C2.

Fig. T.22   BREAKFAST ROOM, JOHN AND JULIA MURPHY RESIDENCE, CA. 1905

JOHN W. AND ANNIE INMAN GRANT'S
SECOND RESIDENCE, CRAIGELLACHIE

WEST PACES FERRY ROAD, 1916

or the Grants' second home, Downing designed a sprawling English country manor house set on 120 acres in the heart of Buckhead. It was said to have been named "Craigellachie" after the Grant family castle in Scotland.[176] The furnishings were a combination of family heirlooms, European and American antiques, and reproductions. The dining room table and chairs were brought from the Grants' first residence on Peachtree Street (figure T.9).

In an article for the *Atlanta Constitution*, May 1916, Isma Dooly highlighted elements of Craigellachie's interior that embodied the changing aesthetic in Atlanta upper-end homes and brought her own evolving design awareness to the society pages. She praised the home's lack of applied ornament, the reliance on an overall design concept, and a thematic unity between interiors and the architectural detailing. In describing the effect of light and vistas visible from the windows, she directed her readers' attention to the relationship of the interior to its exterior setting.

On entering the house, guests deposited coats in the cloakroom and made final adjustments to their appearance in the dressing room before making their formal entrance in the main hall (figure T.23). With its oak-paneled walls, generous fireplace, and plaster-cast ceiling decoration in a Scottish thistle motif, the hall conveys the atmosphere of an exclusive men's club. Three large Eastern rugs cushioned the floor of one of the largest entry halls in Atlanta. Furniture, art, and accessories include two chairs covered in bargello, a "chest cabinet," and a Savonarola chair. An antique painting hangs over the mantel.[177] The library (figure T.24), with its warm, wood-paneled walls and built-in bookcases filled with uniformly bound volumes, is both quietly elegant and inviting. It is furnished with matching sofas of old rose velvet grouped around the fireplace and two chairs upholstered in rose, green, and blue. A painting of Hyde Park by American-born artist Augustus Koopman[178] hangs above the fireplace. "Bright after-dinner repartee, reading, reveries—that is [the library's] atmosphere."[179]

HOUSE
PROUD

[176] William Rudloph, for the Grant-Slaton Collection GS-1, Kenan Research Center, The Atlanta History Center.

[177] "'Craigellachie,' New Country Place of Mr. and Mrs. John W. Grant," *Atlanta Constitution*, 28 May 1916, 3F, 10F.

[178] William Rudloph, for the Grant-Slaton Collection GS-1, Kenan Research Center, The Atlanta History Center. The Augustus Koopman painting is probably "Church Parade in Hyde Park," an illustration of which is found in *The Studio*, 15 June 1907, vol. 41, 225

[179] Medora Field Perkerson, "Grant House Follows Scottish Tradition," *Atlanta Journal Magazine*, 20 May 1923, 13, 20.

Fig. T.23   ENTRY HALL. JOHN W. AND ANNIE GRANT RESIDENCE. CRAIGELLACHIE. CA. 1916

HOUSE
PROUD

Figure 2.11. Dining room, Samuel M. and Mildred McPheeters Inman residence, 1897, Walter T. Downing, architect, F. L. Howe, photographer. W. T. Downing, *Domestic Architecture* (Atlanta: Franklin, 1897), Fred L. Howe Collection, HOW-5-33, Kenan Research Center at the Atlanta History Center.

Figure 2.12. Dining room, Henry B. and Nora Palmer Tompkins residence, (760) Peachtree Street, 1897, Walter T. Downing, architect, F. L. Howe, photographer. W. T. Downing, *Domestic Architecture* (Atlanta: Franklin, 1897), Fred L. Howe Collection, HOW-5-21, Kenan Research Center at the Atlanta History Center.

Figure 2.13. Library, Alfred H. and Sarah Bunn Colquitt, Moreland and Euclid Avenue, ca. 1900, John Moser, architect, F. L. Howe, photographer. Sampson Collection, SMP-1-13, Kenan Research Center at the Atlanta History Center.

Figure 2.14. Bedroom, General John B. and Fanny Haralson Gordon, Sutherland, in Kirkwood, ca. 1895, F. L. Howe, probable photographer. Gen. John B. Gordon Collection, GOR-1-12, Kenan Research Center at the Atlanta History Center.

Figure 2.15. "Old Kitchen," Samuel B. and Helen Reed Turman residence, Hexagon Hall, McDonough Road, ca. 1905. Lethea Lochridge Collection, LOC-1, Kenan Research Center at the Atlanta History Center.

Figure 2.16. Interior illustration, Chamberlin, Boynton & Co., 1879. E. Y. Clark, *Illustrated History of Atlanta* (Atlanta: Jas. P. Harrison & Co. Printers and Binders, 1879). Reprint of second edition, (Atlanta: Cherokee Publishing Company, 1971) 122. Kenan Research Center at the Atlanta History Center.

Figure 2.17. White Hall Street, Atlanta, postcard sent, 1914. Courtesy of Jeff Ashworth.

Figure 2.18. Interior rendering, Walter T. Downing, architect. Walter T. Downing Visual Arts Materials, 1865–1899, VIS 200.028, Kenan Research Center at the Atlanta History Center.

Figure 2.19. Advertisement, Pause, Schroeter & Co. *Architects' Builders' and Hardware Journal* (1/3, January 1890), 38. Kenan Research Center at the Atlanta History Center.

Chapter Three

HOUSE
PROUD

Figure 3.3. Parlor, Henry W. and Julia King Grady residence, (353) Peachtree Street, ca. 1880s, Telamon Cuyler, photographer. Visual Arts Collection, #3349, Kenan Research Center at the Atlanta History Center.

Figure 3.4. Study, Henry W. and Julia King Grady residence, Peachtree Street, ca. 1880s, Telamon Cuyler, photographer. Visual Arts Collection, #3417, Kenan Research Center at the Atlanta History Center.

Figure 3.5. Parlor, Small family residence, East Georgia Avenue, 1889. Visual Arts Collection, #2919, Kenan Research Center at the Atlanta History Center.

Figure 3.6. Entry hall, Frank P. and Mary Mitchell Rice residence, (386) West Peachtree Street, ca. 1890. Rice Family Collection, RIC-1-6, Kenan Research Center at the Atlanta History Center.

Figure 3.7. Parlor, Frank P. and Mary Mitchell Rice residence, ca. 1890. Rice Family Collection, RIC-1-5, Kenan Research Center at the Atlanta History Center.

Figure 3.8. Parlor, unidentified Atlanta home, ca. 1890. Visual Arts Collection, #3962, Kenan Research Center at the Atlanta History Center.

Figure 3.9. Illustration of "Mrs. W. R. Joyner's Japanese Room," *Atlanta Constitution*, 5 December 1897, 9.

Figure 3.10. Interior, Dr. Robinson residence, ca. 1880s. Visual Arts Collection, #1798, Kenan Research Center at the Atlanta History Center.

Figure 3.11. Entry hall, Margie Calhoun residence, Piedmont Road, 1901. *Atlanta Homes: Attractiveness of Residences in the South's Chief City* (Atlanta: Presbyterian Publishing Co., 1901), n.p. Kenan Research Center at the Atlanta History Center.

Figure 3.12. Parlor, Margie Calhoun residence, 1901. *Atlanta Homes: Attractiveness of Residences in the South's Chief City* (Atlanta: Presbyterian Publishing Co., 1901), n.p. Kenan Research Center at the Atlanta History Center.

Figure 3.13. Colonial display window, J. M. High Department Store, 1895, William Whitfield Reynolds, painter and decorator. Visual Arts Collection, #2266, Kenan Research Center at the Atlanta History Center.

Figure 3.14. Colonial Revival furniture advertisement, Chamberlin, Johnson, DuBose Co. *Atlanta Journal*, 16 December 1903, 11.

Figure 3.15. Entry hall, Myra Boynton residence, (272) Rawson Street, 1897, Walter T. Downing, architect, F. L. Howe, photographer. W. T. Downing, *Domestic Architecture* (Atlanta: Franklin, 1897), Fred L. Howe Collection, HOW-4-7, Kenan Research Center at the Atlanta History Center.

Interlude 3

Chapter Four

Figure 4.1. Dining room, Willis E. and Anna Jackson Ragan residence, (574) Peachtree Street, ca. 1911, Edward & Sons, photographers. Visual Arts Collection, #1511, Kenan Research Center at the Atlanta History Center.

Figure 4.2. Parlor, Jack D. Small residence, ca. 1904. Visual Arts Collection #1704, Kenan Research Center at the Atlanta History Center.

Figure 4.3. Bungalow design, 1914, Leila Ross Wilburn, architect. Lelia Ross Wilburn, *Southern Homes and Bungalows* (Atlanta: Privately printed, 1914), 18. Courtesy, Wilburn Collection, Special Collections, McCain Library, Agnes Scott College.

Figure 4.4. Bathroom fixture illustration, 1915. Mme. Maison, "Styles of Bathroom Fixtures May Change, But Best Designs Show Simplicity Makes for Cleanliness," The Housekeeper's Council Table, *Atlanta Constitution Magazine*, 5 December 1915.

Figure 4.5. Interior, Judge Charles W. and Fannie Wright Smith residence, Whiteford Road (later, Oakdale Road), ca. 1912. Daisy Frances Smith Collection, DSM-1-27, Kenan Research Center at the Atlanta History Center.

Figure 4.6. Craftsman furniture advertisement, Chamberlin, Johnson, DuBose Co. *Atlanta Constitution*, 8 December 1909, 6.

Figure 4.7. Grand Rapids furniture advertisement, Empire Furniture Company. *Atlanta Constitution*, 6 September 1914, 12.

Figure 4.8. Dining room, bedroom, and tea room, Frank and Margaret Ladson Adair residence, 1341 South Ponce De Leon Avenue, 1914, Neel Reid, architect. *American Architect*, 11 March 1914. The home is now owned by Paideia School.

Figure 4.9. Entry hall, James L. and Katherine McWhorter Dickey Jr. residence, Arden, 456 West Paces Ferry Road, 1917, Neel Reid, architect, Thurston Hatcher, photographer. Courtesy of Katherine Cox Dickey Marbut.

Figure 4.10. Living room, James L. and Katherine McWhorter Dickey Jr. residence, Arden, 1917, Neel Reid, architect, Thurston Hatcher, photographer. Arden remains a private residence. Courtesy of Katherine Cox Dickey Marbut.

Figure 4.11. Sun room, James L. and Katherine McWhorter Dickey Jr. residence, Arden, 1917, Neel Reid, architect, Thurston Hatcher, photographer. Courtesy of Katherine Cox Dickey Marbut.

Figure 4.12. Dining room, Samuel B. and Helen Reed Turman residence, Hexagon Hall, ca. 1915. Lethea Lochridge Collection, LOC-1-17, Kenan Research Center at the Atlanta History Center.

Figure 4.13. Dining room, Samuel B. and Helen Reed Turman residence, Hexagon Hall, ca. 1915. Lethea Lochridge Collection, LOC-1-16, Kenan Research Center at the Atlanta History Center.

Figure 4.14. Architect's rendering of the great hall, Samuel H. Venable residence, Stonehenge, 1410 Ponce De Leon Avenue, 1913, Edward Emmett Dougherty, architect. "Sam H. Venable's Druid Hills Home Fulfills Dream of Twenty-Five Years," *Atlanta Constitution*, 19 October 1913, 4A. Stonehenge is now the home of St. John's Lutheran Church.

Chapter Five

Figure 5.1. Interior decoration department advertisement, M. Rich & Bros. Department Store, *Atlanta Constitution*, 10 March 1918, 16M.

Figure 5.2. W. E. Browne. Dudley Glass, *Men of Atlanta* (Atlanta: Blosser-Williams Co., 1924), n.p. Kenan Research Center at the Atlanta History Center.

Figure 5.3. W. E. Browne Company's second location, the Studio Building, 1910. *Catalogue of the First Annual Exhibition Held Under the Auspices of the Architectural Arts League of Atlanta and the Atlanta Chapter of the American Institute of Architects* (Atlanta, 1910), n.p. Kenan Research Center at the Atlanta History Center.

Figure 5.4. W. E. Browne Company advertisement, 1910. *Catalogue of the First Annual Exhibition of the Architectural Arts League of Atlanta and the Atlanta Chapter of the American Institute of Architects* (Atlanta: 1910), n.p. Kenan Research Center at the Atlanta History Center.

Figure 5.5. May Belle Clark, 1917, Hirshburg & Clifton, photographers. *Atlanta Constitution Magazine*, 1 April 1917, n.p. http://pqasb.pqarchiver.com/ajc_historic/advancedsearch.html.

Tour of Atlanta Homes

Figure T.1. Entry hall, Richard and Mary Jane Thompson Peters residence, Peachtree Street, between 4th and 5th Streets, ca. 1880s. Peters Album, PET-4-14, (identified in finding aids as the E.C. Peters house) Kenan Research Center at the Atlanta History Center.

Figure T.2. Parlor, Richard and Mary Jane Thompson Peters residence, ca. 1880s. Peters Album, PET-4-14A, (identified in finding aids as the E.C. Peters house) Kenan Research Center at the Atlanta History Center.

Figure T.3. Double parlor, Henry and Sallie Cobb Jackson residence, (111) E. Mitchell Street, ca. 1890. Moore Collection, Moo-1-27A, Kenan Research Center at the Atlanta History Center.

Figure T.4. Dining room, Henry and Sallie Cobb Jackson residence, ca. 1890. Visual Arts Collection #2605, Kenan Research Center at the Atlanta History Center.

Figure T.5. Parlor, John T. and Martha Jackson Grant residence, (427) Peachtree Street, ca. 1898. Grant-Slaton Family Collection, GS-1-14, Kenan Research Center at the Atlanta History Center.

Figure T.6. Vestibule, John W. and Annie Inman Grant, (423) Peachtree Street, 1897, Walter T. Downing, architect, F. L. Howe, photographer. W. T. Downing, *Domestic Architecture* (Atlanta: Franklin, 1897), Visual Arts Collection #1294, Kenan Research Center at the Atlanta History Center.

Figure T.7. Entry hall, John W. and Annie Inman Grant residence, 1897, Walter T. Downing, architect, F. L. Howe, photographer. Grant-Slaton Family Collection, GS-1-28, Kenan Research Center at the Atlanta History Center.

Figure T.8. Reception room, John W. and Annie Inman Grant residence, 1897, Walter T. Downing, architect, F. L. Howe, photographer. W. T. Downing, *Domestic Architecture* (Atlanta: Franklin, 1897), Grant-Slaton Family Collection, GS-1-30, Kenan Research Center at the Atlanta History Center.

Figure T.9. Dining room, John W. and Annie Inman Grant residence, 1897, Walter T. Downing, architect, F. L. Howe, photographer. W. T. Downing, *Domestic Architecture* (Atlanta: Franklin, 1897), Grant-Slaton Family Collection, GS-1-31, Kenan Research Center at the Atlanta History Center.

HOUSE
PROUD

Figure T.21. Dining room, John E. and Julia Gatins Murphy residence, Hillcrest, ca. 1905, Edwards Photography. Katherine John Murphy Riley Collection, RIL-3-1, Kenan Research Center at the Atlanta History Center.

Figure T.22. Breakfast room, John E. and Julia Gatins Murphy residence, Hillcrest, ca. 1905, Edwards Photography. Katherine John Murphy Riley Collection, RIL-4-1, Kenan Research Center at the Atlanta History Center.

Figure T.23. Entry Hall, John W. and Annie Inman Grant residence, Craigellachie, 155 West Paces Ferry Road, ca.1916, Walter T. Downing, architect. Craigellachie is now the Cherokee Town and Country Club. Grant-Slaton Family Collection, GS-2-15, Kenan Research Center at the Atlanta History Center.

Figure T.24. Library, John W. and Annie Inman Grant Residence, Craigellachie, ca. 1916, Walter T. Downing, architect. Grant-Slaton Family Collection, GS-2-20, Kenan Research Center at the Atlanta History Center.